About the Author

Veteran prairie journalist Verne Clemence was born in Kindersley in western Saskatchewan in 1937 and raised on a farm in the Kindersley district. He gave up on his dream to become a farmer after contracting polio in his early teens. He got into journalism after working at a variety of administrative jobs and became editor of the *Kindersley Clarion*, a weekly newspaper, in the 1960s. He moved to Yorkton in 1969 to work on another weekly, the *Yorkton Enterprise*, and then joined the *Saskatoon StarPhoenix* in 1972. Since taking early retirement in 1996, he has operated his own writing and editing business from home. Clemence has been a book reviewer for many years and continues to write a book column for the *StarPhoenix*. *Saskatchewan's Own* is his second book. He is also the author of the biography *David M. Baltzan: Prairie Doctor*, published in 1995 by Fitzhenry & Whiteside. Clemence lives in Saskatoon with his wife Miriam. They have two adult children, Crystal and Greg, and live with a bossy Bo   nd a diabetic calico cat called Sassy.

To all those whose vision, courage, and hard work created
the legacy we enjoy in Saskatchewan today

Saskatchewan's Own

PEOPLE WHO MADE A DIFFERENCE

Verne Clemence

FIFTH
HOUSE

Cover and interior design by Kathy Aldous-Schleindl
Cover background photo by John Perret
Cover inset photos (clockwise from top left): Archie Belaney (Grey Owl), Yousuf Karsh/National Archives of Canada/PA-195789; Sandra Schmirler, Sandra Schmirler Foundation; Tommy Douglas, Len Hillyard, Saskatchewan Archives Board R-B2876-1; Mistahimusqua (Big Bear), Glenbow Archives NA-2306-2; W. O. Mitchell, Deborah MacNeill, W.O. Mitchell fonds, Special Collections, University of Calgary Library; Geraldine Moodie, Glenbow Archives NA-1315-18
Title page photos (left to right): Sophia Dixon, Saskatchewan Archives Board S-B5517; David Baltzan, Baltzan family; Mattie Mayes, Saskatchewan Archives Board R-A7691
Edited by Eilish Hiebert
Copyedited by Meaghan Craven
Proofread by Joan Tetrault
Scans by St. Solo Computer Graphics

Canada Council   Conseil des Arts
for the Arts   du Canada

The publisher gratefully acknowledges the support of The Canada Council for the Arts and the Department of Canadian Heritage. We acknowledge the financial support of the Government of Canada through the Book Publishing Industry Development Program (BPIDP) for our publishing activities.

Printed in Canada by Friesens
04 05 06 07 08/ 5 4 3 2 1
First published in the United States in 2004

National Library of Canada Cataloguing in Publication Data
Clemence, Verne, 1937-
      Saskatchewan's own : people who made a difference / Verne Clemence.
      Includes bibliographical references and index.
      ISBN 1-894004-90-6
      1. Saskatchewan—Biography. 2. Saskatchewan—History—Miscellanea. I. Title.
FC3505.C54 2004   971.24'009'9   C2003-907136-7

Fifth House Ltd.   Fitzhenry & Whiteside
A Fitzhenry & Whiteside Company   121 Harvard Avenue, Suite 2
1511-1800 4 St. SW   Allston, MA, 02134
Calgary, AB, T2S 2S5
1-800-387-9776
www.fitzhenry.ca

Contents

Introduction

Saskatchewan's story for its first one hundred years is a people story. The movers and shakers, the not so visible, the obscure—they all played a part in creating a province that is similar to its neighbours, but also unique in many important ways. A combination of necessity and idealism spawned an enduring co-operative movement in Saskatchewan. The same forces were behind the creation of a health care system whose twin principles of affordability and accessibility ultimately set the standard for all of Canada. The people of Saskatchewan also created a groundbreaking network of social services aimed at mitigating the extreme poverty of the years of the Great Depression. Education was accorded a high priority, to the point that degrees from the province's two universities are now recognized and respected all over the world. Similarly, a strong arts community has grown out of the diverse cultural influences in the province, encouraged by programs of public support that started sixty years ago. Saskatchewan writers, performers, and visual artists routinely earn recognition far beyond the province's borders.

But maintaining a system rooted in a belief in an egalitarian society has been a challenge. The one constant in Saskatchewan over its first one hundred years has been change. From massive immigration in the early part of the century—as the settling of the Great Plains followed the arrival of the railroad—through mechanization of farming, and followed by post-war industrialization and the onset of rural depopulation, the province seems to have been in a permanent state of flux for most of its existence. One of the greatest disruptions occurred during the Great Depression of the 1930s as Saskatchewan bore the brunt of the lethal combination of economic stagnation and four- to five-year drought. It was a time when the conventional became suspect and institutions such as banks and grain companies, once cornerstones of the prairie economy, came to be regarded as oppressors. Desperate farmers, small business operators, and labourers made common cause and defied these symbols of Bay Street colonization. They demanded better prices for their grain, more jobs, and a better approach to the needs of businesses for capital to ride out the bad years. They succeeded in shaking up the federal government, but in broadcasting their plight far and wide they made the investment community nervous, creating a problem for the Saskatchewan government in the recovery period. If Saskatchewan was going to truly safeguard itself from similar disasters in the future, the newly minted CCF (Co-operative Commonwealth Federation), with the preacher-politician Tommy Douglas in the premier's chair, had to sell investors on the viability of industrial development in a sparsely populated province, far from markets. All the while, Saskatchewan politicians had to preserve the social system that had come to define the province, or face the wrath of the electorate. Politicians of all stripes who tried to break with the past and become more business-oriented have paid the price.

The beat goes on. Political and ideological debate in Saskatchewan has always been lively and deeply polarized. No doubt it will stay that way. The passions of citizens from all walks of life inform that debate, as befits a province once likened by its most famous orator, Tommy Douglas, to "a new Jerusalem."

Saskatchewan is more than just a social laboratory, of course. Over the years its people have found ways to grow crops where rainfall is consistently low; to develop strains of wheat that overcame such problems as early frost, sawfly, and rust; to divert waterways to make dry areas blossom; and to become significant players in mining, forestry, and the petroleum industry.

The sweeping changes that have taken place in the province of Saskatchewan have required strong political leadership. Representative of their ranks in this book are some of Saskatchewan's strongest leaders, such as Walter Scott, the province's first premier and hands down its most outspoken booster. Scott came to office in 1905 proclaiming to one and all that Saskatchewan was destined for greatness, and would surely one day have a population of no less than ten million. Douglas, of course, was the great reformer and unquestionably Saskatchewan's most revered premier. John Diefenbaker made his mark at the federal level, bursting onto the national scene as prime minister with the biggest majority in the history of the country. Another noted visionary, he proved to be the master of promoting his ideas, but failed when it came to implementing them.

Picking the few names of the people who made a difference in Saskatchewan's first hundred years was the easiest part about writing this book. What I quickly discovered was that there are hundreds, maybe thousands, of men and women whose contributions are worthy of our attention, and our appreciation. These are the people who created our institutions, our towns and cities, our hospitals, schools, and libraries. They were leaders in the arts and sciences, individuals who excelled at sports, or perhaps worked in the background for the betterment of youth. Scores of dedicated people worked tirelessly to bring about greater stability in agriculture through co-operatives. And the story needed another aspect as well, found in the lives of those who listened to their own drums—a farmer who secretly recorded the life of his community in verse; another who built an ocean-going sailing vessel in the midst of a sea of dry land; a loner with a passion for finding dinosaur bones in southern Saskatchewan. In their own ways each of them added colour and texture to the fabric of life in the province.

So what follows in this book came about through a purely subjective process. I grew up in Saskatchewan and I've lived here most of my life so I relied on my own observations in making my selections.

I did have a great deal of help, however, from almost every area of the province, from people who suggested names, and for that I am most grateful. The research material came from many sources, with the local history room in the Saskatoon Public Library playing a large role. The Internet was a good friend in this kind of endeavour too, as were helpful friends who gave me odd bits of information, and others who went out of their way to be helpful. A list of the books I used in carrying out research for *Saskatchewan's Own* appears in the list of references. Most are available on the shelves of Canadian libraries, and I highly recommend them to anyone wanting to know more about the individuals I wrote about, or about Saskatchewan history. I am indebted to all these authors for the work they have done to bring pieces of our past to life.

Also, I would be remiss if I didn't express my deep appreciation to Fifth House, and especially to Lesley Reynolds who has patiently and with great professionalism seen this project through with me.

Most of all I want to thank my wife Miriam for all the research she did. There wouldn't have been a book without her help and support.

For my part, this venture has reaffirmed my belief that we have a rich and fascinating history in Saskatchewan, and we've only touched the surface so far.

Verne Clemence

Educator, Statesman

GRANT MACEWAN

1902–2000

Grant MacEwan during his term as mayor of Calgary, 1963–65.

No doubt each of the three prairie provinces could find good reason to claim the legendary Grant MacEwan as its own. Alberta, especially, has adopted the one-time Calgary mayor and flamboyant lieutenant governor as one of its citizens of great distinction. He was that, of course, but what is less widely known is that MacEwan spent his formative years in Saskatchewan, and later left an indelible mark as one of the province's leading academics. From 1928 to 1946, during his term as professor of animal husbandry at the University of Saskatchewan, Grant Mac-Ewan created an unprecedented rapport between rural and urban dwellers, advanced his progressive ideas about raising livestock, and worked as volunteer head of the Saskatoon exhibition. He also travelled the province regularly to serve as a judge in live-stock shows, and to promote the cause of education in the all-important agriculture industry.

Farming was in Grant MacEwan's blood. Born near Brandon, Manitoba, in 1902 into a farming family of Scottish ancestry, he came to Saskatchewan as a pre-teen when his father, Alexander, a restless and somewhat impulsive man in his younger days, bought a piece of land—sight unseen—in the Melfort area. The seller had promised a great deal, including a full set of buildings, a herd of cattle, and fully broken fields ready to seed. But when Alexander and young Grant arrived to get everything ready for the rest of the family—Grant's mother Bertha and younger brother George—they discovered that they had been hood-winked. The land was a big slough, mostly under water, and there was nothing else.

But the die was cast. MacEwan senior had sold the family farm in Manitoba and there was nothing to go back to. So he took the last of his money, found another piece of land with an old granary on it, and set about trying to make a livable place for his wife and sons. Mrs. Bertha MacEwan, a tough-minded and conservative woman, had lived a life of comfort, if not privilege, and she was not amused. The family's fortunes took another dip when they lost their first crop to rust and had barely enough food to survive the winter. But they persevered, not in the least because of young Grant's resourcefulness. From an early age he had demonstrated an entrepreneurial spirit. Back in Brandon he had built up a bank account of $50 (a considerable sum of money in those days) by selling the excess milk and cream from the family cow to his town neighbours. He lived too far from Melfort to do the same thing in his new home, but he did go into partnership with his father, buying a cow and selling her calves. Eventually the MacEwans did manage to harvest a good crop, build a new house, and turn their farm into a money-making enterprise.

Grant and his brother walked to school in Melfort and worked on the farm. That was all Grant really wanted until at the end of high school he became interested in extending his education. He attended the Ontario College of Agriculture, where he graduated with a Bachelor of Science in agriculture in 1926, and then obtained a Master of Science at Ohio State College in 1928. He always made it back to the farm to help with seeding and harvest, but between 1924 and 1928 he focused on either attending classes, or finding part-time work to finance his fees, books, and living expenses.

The MacEwans were touched by tragedy while Grant was away at college. His younger brother George contracted meningitis and died in the fall of 1924. Alexander and Bertha were devastated. Grant came home immediately, staying to help with the harvest and trying to help his parents through their time of grief. He was also torn between his wish to finish his master's degree and their need for him on the farm, but with their blessing, he eventually went back to school.

MacEwan had made a name for himself in two years at Ohio State, and as graduation approached he began to receive job offers. Eventually he accepted the position of chief assistant to the live stock commissioner with the Saskatchewan government, but shortly after that his dream offer came in a telegram from the University of Saskatchewan where his services were sought as assistant professor of animal husbandry. After some soul searching, he reneged on his letter of acceptance to the government and returned to Saskatchewan to plunge into the career that would preoccupy him for the next period of his life. As a true son of the soil, MacEwan brought a whole new approach to the role of university professor. Of course he looked after his responsibilities as a teacher, giving the requisite lectures and attending meetings, but Grant also concentrated on the practical side of farming. MacEwan realized, as few others did in academe, that in addition to conducting research and honing new theories, academics could provide farmers with needed advice and information that they could put to practical use.

Having seen the worst that Saskatchewan weather could dish out, and understanding the vagaries of the agriculture industry, MacEwan knew when help was needed and how to give hope when spirits were low. That approach was to be especially important through the grinding years of drought and poverty during the Great Depression. Saskatoon wasn't in the worst drought area, but MacEwan travelled the whole province and was well aware of the devastation. Indeed, the crops he was overseeing on university land were hit as hard as any. There was no harvest at all for two years of the 1930s, and for a further two years the yield dropped from the usual twenty-five-plus bushels per acre to below five.

It was during those desperate years that MacEwan started the writing career that would eventually become a full-time occupation. Writing came easily to MacEwan. He regularly turned out academic papers during his university years, but it wasn't until the 1930s that he became interested in writing books. The first two were textbooks. MacEwan and his friend and colleague Al Ewen had long been concerned about a lack of agricultural textbooks, so they decided to try to fill the gap. Their efforts succeeded beyond their expectations and their books quickly became popular. MacEwan was so devoted to the textbook project that he was still revising one of the manuscripts on his honeymoon.

Grant MacEwan was a devout man, a churchgoer who sang in the choir, a teetotaler, and a non-smoker. He was tall, exceptionally well built, and very fit. It was while singing in the United Church choir that Grant met Phyllis Cline, a young woman from Churchbridge in the eastern part of the province, who also sang in the choir. Phyllis was a teacher in Saskatoon at the time. Grant and Phyllis married in 1931.

In addition to two textbooks he wrote with Ewen, MacEwan wrote one more on his own, and then went on to broaden his horizons, writing for both academic periodicals and newspapers aimed at the farm audience. Grant MacEwan had a lifelong interest in outdoor activities and in the natural world. His years at the University of Saskatchewan were marked by a heightened interest in conservation, especially conservation of the soil of western Canada. His writings from that period demonstrate a kind of commitment to ecology that put him well before his time. But it was his reputation in the farming community that led people to trust MacEwan, and to take seriously his often-repeated concerns about soil erosion and farming practices that encouraged the degradation of the land.

MacEwan also ventured into the arena of public speaking during those years in Saskatchewan. He became a popular speaking guest at farm meetings around the province, and soon service clubs in the city were inviting him to give talks to their memberships. He also became a regular on the radio, promoting conservation and discussing his theories on farming practices. MacEwan had ideas that seemed revolutionary at the time, and he was a passionate orator. He urged farmers to stop plowing deeply in their summerfallowing operations, to leave plant material on the surface to guard against soil erosion from wind and water. Capping the soil sealed in moisture as well, which fit in with his second priority, conservation of water. In those days before television, even non-farmers attended his talks and lectures, as much for the entertainment value as for the information.

Small wonder that, as Grant MacEwan acquired a high public profile, political parties began to cast eyes his way. A lifelong Liberal, following his father's footsteps, Grant had a keen interest in political affairs, but didn't feel the timing was right when he was invited to become a Liberal candidate in a provincial election. In due course he was pursued by both Liberals and Conservatives, federal and provincial, and even offered the leadership of the Saskatchewan Liberal party, but he stuck to his guns. He wasn't ready to jump into the political arena. He still had goals to achieve in academic life, for one thing, and he still felt that he needed to live longer, to experience more things, before he entered politics.

It wasn't until the postwar years and a series of changes at the university that Grant took a serious look at life in politics. Changes in the top administrative posts at the university meant that MacEwan's approach to his job was suddenly out of favour. The university was trying to redirect the focus of the agricultural department toward more scientific research and away from what they thought of as the "folksy" approach MacEwan had developed. MacEwan continued to spend time on his volunteer work in the country, but his bosses were making it clear that it was without their blessing. In 1946, the University of Manitoba offered him the post of dean of the College of Agriculture. It was a long-held dream to become dean, and he had been passed over at the University of Saskatchewan.

There was nothing left to hold MacEwan in Saskatchewan. His parents, wishing to retire, had offered the family farm to him in 1941. He was attracted by the sentimental value of the land, but little else, and he refused. The old homestead went on the auction block and was sold that same year. Grant's mother, Bertha MacEwan, died in 1944, and his father, Alex, died eleven months later. Grant's wife, Phyllis, favoured the move to Manitoba, so he accepted the deanship. It was in Manitoba that Grant MacEwan made his first try for political office. That was a disappointing failure, and the MacEwans were soon on the move again. Grant had invested in a piece of land at Priddis, not far from Calgary, and he decided to build a home there and devote himself to writing. That didn't actually happen quite as planned, but it did mark the beginning of a whole new chapter of MacEwan's life.

Grant MacEwan's exploits in Alberta are well documented,

and his writing career that produced over fifty books on western Canadian history bears its own testament to his many accomplishments. But his early years in Saskatchewan were vital both to the man MacEwan would become and to the future success of an appreciative agriculture industry.

After those formative years in Saskatchewan, Grant MacEwan went on to become mayor of Calgary, lieutenant governor of Alberta, and University of Calgary professor. He lived out his years in Calgary, with a prolific writing career that continued right up until his death in 2000 at the age of ninety-seven.

The Sad Giant

EDOUARD BEAUPRÉ

1881–1904

At 2.5 metres tall, Edouard Beaupré, the Willow
Bunch Giant, towered over his peers.

*O*ne of Saskatchewan's most enduring legends is also one of its saddest stories. The short life of Edouard Beaupré, also known as the Willow Bunch Giant, became one of those tales that defined the image of the province here and abroad during the early years of the twentieth century.

Beaupré's story is one of shocking exploitation that was nothing short of cruelty. But, like the treatment accorded the Dionne quintuplets in the 1930s and 1940s in eastern Canada, it was typical of the times. Thankfully, the notion of publicly displaying people who are different—for any reason—is now recognized as a violation of rights, to say nothing of violating dignity and common sense. That doesn't mean that such things don't still happen, but almost certainly the tragic chain of events that lead to Edouard Beaupré's untimely death, far from home and from anyone who cared for him, could not be duplicated today.

Edouard started out his life as a normal—if rather large— baby, the first of twenty children born to Gaspard Beaupré and his Métis wife, Florestine. Edouard's parents were both quite tall, but not extraordinarily so. All of his siblings were normal in their growth patterns, and, for the first few years, Edouard's growth seemed normal as well. However, at age four Edouard's pace increased, and he towered over his peers by the time he started school. At age nine he was close to two metres tall. A sensitive and intelligent lad, Edouard's size was an embarrassment. He felt isolated and often bore the brunt of the cruel humour of the schoolyard.

The Beaupré's lived in the ranching country of the south. Young Edouard was fascinated by the cowboy life. It was his dream to follow that life, so he quit school at age fifteen— education was not highly valued anyway—and found a job as a ranch hand. But he kept growing. Within two years Edouard literally outgrew his job. At 136 kilograms and over the 2-metre mark, he was too much of a load for the range ponies that were the workhorses of the prairies. Also, because his feet were dragging on the ground it was no longer possible to fit him with a saddle. Back home, with no means of making his living, Edouard could only work on the Beaupré's small farm. But with such a large family it was difficult at the best of times, and with a son of Edouard's size and dimensions, just housing him was a problem. Regular-sized beds were useless to him. It was even difficult for him to go in and out of doors, or sit comfortably at a table to consume the large portions of food needed to keep him going. And that wasn't all—Edouard was still growing.

It was a family friend at Willow Bunch who first suggested that the outsized man should turn his size into profit by getting into the freak show business. A display in Barnum's American Museum in New York gives some background to this unsavory business:

> For 100 years (1840–1940) the freak show was one of America's most popular forms of entertainment. Today the same shows would be considered unacceptable and cruel, or as one disability rights activist put it, 'the pornography of disability.' In the mid 19th century, however, Americans were beginning to move from the farms and a family-based society to one which relied more on organizations, including institutionalized entertainment. It was at this time that P.T. Barnum brought the freak show to prominence.

Who knows what Edouard himself thought of the idea, but he was huge compared to anyone else he knew, and he was also exceptionally strong. Indeed, his feats of strength were already becoming legendary around Saskatchewan. And having lived a relatively sheltered life that didn't involve travel, he would have no way of knowing how dehumanizing it would be to be put on display, promoted as a freak of nature. The idea took hold, however, especially when the proponents pointed out that

Edouard could make his own living and send money home to support the rest of the family by touring as the Willow Bunch Giant, the name that would become his for the rest of his short life.

Edouard felt obligated to try to capitalize on his size and attempt to turn it to his advantage. So he set off, accompanied by two neighbour men who would be his managers. He was seventeen, and no doubt filled with apprehension. Edouard's handlers organized an ambitious tour that would take him to Winnipeg and Montreal in Canada, and a number of cities in the United States, from Buffalo in the north to California in the south. Edouard soon acquired an agent and had regular work touring with a circus.

At twenty-one years of age, Edouard was 2.5 metres tall and weighed about 180 kilograms. He was well proportioned and trim, but he stood out like a sore thumb and attracted rude stares wherever he went. Family lore has it that his shoe size was twenty-two, his hat size fifteen, and it took almost 6.4 metres of fabric to make one of the custom-made shirts he needed. The sleeves were 1.2 metres long.

Touring meant more than just being ogled by curious crowds. Edouard also wrestled with powerful and well-trained opponents, using only his size and strength against their superior technique. He also performed feats of strength. Lifting was one of his main attractions. For example, he would crouch under a 360-kilogram horse that was standing on a platform and carry the animal on his back. He was on the road incessantly, seldom out of the public eye. It was a lonely, stressful life. The travel was all by train in the cruel glare of probing gazes of the curious. He could barely fit himself into the seats on the train, and the hotel rooms that were his only respite weren't much better. All anybody could do for him was to put a steamer trunk at the end of the bed so he had somewhere to rest his feet. He was beginning to get a permanent stoop from bending to get through doorways wherever he went.

To make matters even worse, Edouard saw little or nothing of the money his tours were bringing in. According to later reports very little ever found its way back to his family either, leading to the conclusion that his exploiters were pocketing the profits. Doubtless they were a worried lot when their meal ticket, Edouard, became ill from the life he was leading. In 1904 he was diagnosed with tuberculosis. He worked as long as he could stay on his feet, but he finally died two years later while performing at the St. Louis World's Fair with the Barnum and Bailey Circus. His six years of misery on the freak show circuit were over. The Willow Bunch Giant was dead, at only twenty-three years.

The battles of various family members to bring the body home for a decent burial had just begun, however. Neither his employer nor his agent would put anything toward the cost of shipping the body, and Gaspard Beaupré ran out of money at Winnipeg when he tried to travel to St. Louis to bring Edouard home. As a result the body fell into the hands of medical researchers in the United States. They determined that Edouard's growth problem was due to a malfunctioning pituitary gland. Amazingly, he was still growing when he died.

Edouard Beaupré's agent claimed the corpse after the pathologists had made their examination. He had it embalmed and put it on display again, ostensibly to make enough money to pay for the embalming and send Edouard home. Somehow, the body ended up in a Montreal museum a year later, followed by another ghoulish round of freak show appearances. Eventually, the body was put on display at the University of Montreal.

It wasn't until almost seventy years later that Edouard's remains were finally claimed by relatives and returned to Willow Bunch for burial, thus ending his bizarre story, one of the most poignant from Saskatchewan's past.

A Woman for All Seasons

DIANA KINGSMILL WRIGHT

1908–1982

Diana Kingsmill, shown here in the 1930s, was "a genuine
Canadian eccentric" in the words of film star David Niven.

*D*iana Kingsmill Wright left her mark in two worlds during a long and productive life. As the Upper Canada daughter of a much honoured and decorated admiral in the Royal Navy, the vivacious and attractive young Diana was sent to boarding school in England to learn how to be a lady. Among other things, that meant schooling in the art of decorating ballrooms with her presence, and becoming adept at riding sidesaddle. She participated in the British ritual of riding to hounds and fell in love with skiing on frequent holidays in the Swiss Alps. She returned to Ottawa in 1929 and was a debutante. Home was a mansion run by servants, and her life focused on the social whirl of the city, along with the pursuit of her passion for skiing. She was also an accomplished figure skater and equestrian.

In 1932, she met and married Victor Gordon-Lennox, an Englishman several years her senior, who was on assignment in Canada as a diplomatic correspondent for the *London Telegraph*. She returned with him to London, where she became a popular hostess between trips to the capitals of Europe, when she accompanied her husband, who was often sent abroad to cover the events of the day. She moved in the top social circles in London, befriending the movers and shakers of the city. Film star David Niven recalled Diana in his memoirs, calling her "a rarity—a genuine Canadian eccentric. Dark, with beautiful teeth and a lovely smile, she was highly intelligent, smoked small cigars and wore a monocle." The monocle became a trademark for the independent Diana, and even played a part in introducing her to her second husband.

Most summers saw her back in Canada with her son George to enjoy the Kingsmill's summer home on Grindstone Island on the picturesque Big Rideau Lake, not far from Ottawa. It was a summer getaway on a grand scale, with servants to look after every need. She moved in the top social circles and her skiing prowess was well known.

Diana was pressed into service as a member of Canada's ski-racing team in the 1936 Olympics. Governments did not have the money to assist their athletes in the depressed 1930s, so only those who had the resources to pay their own way took part. However, given Diana's prodigious skills, it's entirely possible that she would have made the team on merit. Unfortunately, she fractured a bone in her hand shortly before the big race, and though she competed with the cast removed and the hand taped to the ski pole, the injury held her back and the team did not win. The performance was typical of the determined woman. She may have been prepared by birth and training to take the road of least resistance, but Diana did not back away from a challenge. Considering the turn her life was about to take, that trait stood her in good stead.

With war clouds gathering over much of Europe in 1939, and her marriage about to end in divorce, Diana returned to Ottawa. She went to work for the Health League of Canada, and in her spare time she set up displays encouraging victory gardens and sound nutrition. During this period, Diana actually came close to preparing food. As a young woman growing up in a household filled with efficient servants, she hadn't even been allowed to go into the kitchen.

Diana's social life continued to be active during the 1940s, and it was at one of the regular parties she attended that she met Jim Wright. Jim was a reporter and writer from Saskatchewan with a reputation as a crusading prairie socialist. His book *Slava Bohu, Story of the Doukhobors*, had earned him a Governor General's Award in 1940. Wright's fondest hope was to draw attention to the plight of prairie farmers who were still struggling to throw off the effects of the devastating years of depression in the 1930s. When he met Diana, Jim Wright was working for the National Film Board, but he told her his real profession was as a stoker on a ship, a job he had actually worked at for a time. Diana thought he was joking. Years later she recalled that he asked her point blank, "Why do you wear that funny thing in your eye?" referring, of course, to the ever-present monocle. She explained that when she was skiing her eyes would water, and it was easy to wipe the single lens on her sleeve and have at least one good eye to find her way down the slopes. "The next night he phoned and asked me to go for a walk. Nobody had ever asked me to go for a walk before, so I went. Of course he didn't have any money to ask me anywhere else."

The two were married soon after that. Jim Wright took Diana back to his home province of Saskatchewan, to live in an abandoned farmhouse in the Landis area. It must have been a shock to the woman who had once rubbed shoulders with the rich and famous, but by all accounts she took to life without electricity or plumbing, quickly adapting to wood-burning stoves and hauling water from a nearby well. Jim was busy trying to eke out a living as a freelance writer, working for the *StarPhoenix* in Saskatoon, or any other newspaper or periodical that would pay for his services. He also wrote books, but received little in return for much hard work. Meanwhile, he pursued his interest in the problems of his farming neighbours.

Diana helped with his work. She had learned to type some years earlier, and she put the knowledge to good use. She also helped with research and editing. Her son George joined the couple when his term at boarding school ended, and some time later Jim and Diana had another son, Dane. The small family moved to Saskatoon, settling in a small farmhouse on a twelve-hectare site just south of the city. The Wrights were a popular couple, and their home became a focal point for regular gatherings of like-minded people who wanted to make changes in the world. Diana, ever the accomplished hostess, had to quickly learn the basics of cooking. She taught herself a few staple recipes, and became known as an innovative cook who never turned a guest away at mealtime.

Jim started a small newspaper, *Union Farmer*, about a year after their move. It quickly became the focus of both their lives, steadily gaining a national reputation as the liveliest farm publication to emerge from the prairies in many years. Diana soon assumed the mantle of acting editor, and later editor, as the work became full time. The work absorbed her for about seven years and expanded her knowledge of prairie agriculture and politics, as well as the co-operative movement, a powerful force that swept the prairie provinces in that era.

Diana moved on to take on an active role in the Voice of Women in the 1960s, and became a high-profile advocate for a more egalitarian society. After her parents died, she was instrumental in converting the Kingsmill's summer home on Rideau Lake into a centre for peace studies.

After Jim died suddenly in 1970, Diana took some time to grieve and adjust, then turned her attention to the problems besetting the environment. She had been interested in environmental issues since the 1950s, but her work with other causes kept her from taking an active role. Diana volunteered to take over the editorial duties of *Environment Probe*, a Saskatchewan-based magazine, and soon made the publication a must-read for anyone interested in preserving the environment. She helped organize conferences on soil-conserving farming methods and served as a member of CBC Radio's agricultural advisory committee, always working to make sure conservation of the soil was not ignored. A citation for an award she received a year before her death perfectly captures her life's work: "Diana Wright's life is a testament to her belief in the need for humankind to live in harmony with nature ... her openness to new ideas, her supportiveness and warm hospitality have provided an atmosphere in which people have grown, explored and found encouragement." Thus Diana Wright, former Upper Canada socialite, later prairie wife, mother, and activist, left her mark on Saskatchewan.

The Bone Man

CORKY JONES

1880–1978

Harold Saunders (Corky) Jones was Saskatchewan's first paleontologist.

*M*any individuals laboured in relative obscurity during the nineteenth and twentieth centuries as they made their unique contributions to the building of the province of Saskatchewan. Most of the amateurs and scientists who were the province's first paleontologists, such as Harold Saunders (Corky) Jones, neither sought nor wanted public acclaim. Jones was obsessed with paleontology and the hunt for artifacts of the past, and he wanted to pass on to others the things he learned. He accomplished much, but the true significance of his work wasn't recognized until after his death.

Jones had visited fossil beds on the Isle of Wight with his father when he was a child in England. Because of that experience he developed an interest in paleontology. Although Corky never did have any formal training, he was a "bone hound" with a keen eye for fertile ground. When he immigrated to Canada in 1898, he ended up in the Eastend area, a patch of land tucked away in a corner of what was then the North-West Territories. (Ironically, Eastend is in southwestern Saskatchewan—at the east end of the Cypress Hills.) After a cursory look around at the landscape, the bone hound in Jones immediately recognized the signs of fossil country, and he decided to stay for a while. The while turned into a lifetime, during which he proved his assessment of the area to be accurate.

There aren't many records of those early years, but it is known that Corky Jones landed a job as a greenhorn cowboy on a ranch near Eastend. Just how his fellow cowboys regarded his peculiar habit of poking around for old bones in the coulees of the vast ranching country is not known, but it isn't hard to imagine. Only a few outsiders had done anything like that before, so without doubt, he would have been regarded at best as an eccentric.

Jones was undeterred, however, and in the years to come his

interest grew, as did his list of finds. He studied whatever literature he could find on paleontology but that wasn't much in a small town far from any academic outposts. But he kept searching, and digging, and learning as he went along. In the early 1920s, he met a soul mate in the person of Charles Sternberg, the son of a famed fossil hunter from eastern Canada. Sternberg was a surveyor for the Geological Society of Canada who happened to be passing through Eastend. He saw one of the bones Jones had discovered, and had managed to mount for a display. Sternberg recognized the piece as a significant find that proved the presence of beds of the Lance age in an area where they were not previously known. He sought Jones out, and so began a relationship that lasted many years and advanced Corky's work. The two were in touch frequently, mostly through an exchange of letters. Through Sternberg, Jones received needed help, information, and study materials. Contact with Sternberg marked a turning point for the determined amateur.

Identification was the principal problem Jones faced, and Sternberg was an authority he could turn to. A letter from Sternberg in 1931 demonstrates just how important Sternberg's help was to his friend Corky Jones. "I am returning today, under separate cover, the bone which you sent me for identification … it is an ungula phalanx or claw bone of a large carnivorous dinosaur, Tyrannosaurus rex." It wasn't until some sixty years later, with the discovery of the intact T. rex fossil near Eastend—dubbed "Scotty" by many Saskatchewan residents—that the significance of Jones's work came into focus.

Jones didn't make any money in his pursuit of old bones. In the 1930s, the Town of Eastend employed him. Among his duties was that of town constable, and his unusual approach to traffic control attracted the attention of another of his paleontologist friends, Dr. Loris Russell, an employee of the National Museum of Canada. In a letter in remembrance of his old friend, Russell wrote: "I recall when he was town constable and had installed a wooden post in the main intersection to dissuade vehicles from cutting corners. This was known as Corky's police force. On

Sunday morning, when it was found leaning at an inebriate angle, this dereliction of duty would be gravely reported to 'the Chief.' "The post was, in fact, an old Coca-Cola sign, which had been redesigned to depict a policeman in uniform. Corky Jones was much better at finding dinosaurs than directing traffic.

In 1936, Jones reported another significant find to Sternberg—a partial Triceratops skull. And, in the 1940s, even though there had been a lull in his work during the Second World War, and in spite of some health problems, Corky was back in the field, making a discovery in the Frenchman River Valley that attracted the interest of both the provincial government and the University of Saskatchewan. It was at this time that he hired himself out as a guide to an increasing number of visitors interested in the Eastend area.

Toward the end of the 1940s, Corky Jones began to look for a way to display his many finds, and found what he thought would be a secure home. He created his own personal museum in the basement of the old Eastend School, doing all the work himself. It was soon regarded as the best personal collection of dinosaur bones in western Canada, and perhaps the whole country. However, tragedy struck in 1952 when the Frenchman River overflowed its banks and flooded the town. Some items in Corky's museum were lost and many were damaged, but with the help of volunteers from the community, and from the National Museum of Canada and the Saskatchewan Museum of Natural History, most of the collection was saved and put into a display in the new Eastend School. It has been moved since that time to the Pastime Theatre.

Jones's work did a lot to put the Eastend area on Canada's fossil map, and in 1972 his name also found its way onto the Saskatchewan map when Jones' Peak, overlooking the Frenchman River, was named in his honour. In the 1980s, the Eastend Tourism Board began the planning that resulted in the construction of a world-class paleontology centre in the Frenchman River Valley near the town, and work continues on other displays. The project got a big boost with the discovery of the T. rex fossil near Eastend in 1994. Work continues to go on at that site to unearth the rest of the skeleton. Corky Jones would have been enthralled with it all, and hopefully he would have appreciated the memorials to his work that are on prominent display in many places, including at the Pastime Theatre, Eastend, Saskatchewan.

Corky Jones died in 1978, apparently still in the relative obscurity he had preferred throughout most of his life. And while his life's work is enshrined in new buildings and glittering displays, the true essence of the man was captured in the words of Wallace Stegner in his acclaimed book *Wolf Willow*: "He is nobody important—an old-timer who lives in a little three-room house near the centre of town and probably never made two hundred dollars a month in his life ... he has never scorned learning, he has always been willing to try importing it."

A Legend in the Water

HARRY BAILEY

1913–2000

Harry Bailey talking to a group of young swimmers at poolside in Saskatoon.

n Saskatchewan, and in competitive swimming circles far beyond, he was known as the patriarch of the pool. Yet Harry Bailey, who coached swimmers all the way from kiddies' classes to Olympic contenders, never had a lesson in coaching, or for that matter, in swimming technique. He was self-taught and self-motivated, with a reputation for extraordinary dedication to the sport he loved.

The hundreds of people who benefited from Harry Bailey's teaching remember him as a disciplinarian who pushed them to the limit, but they also recall his dry sense of humour. One of his favourite yarns was how he became a competitive swimmer because he didn't have a pair of skates as a child. Another one was about almost drowning in the Dog-Eyed River—a small waterway near Tisdale that only had water in spring and early summer.

Harry Bailey was twelve years old when his family moved to Saskatoon. One day, while visiting the Riversdale Swimming Pool, somebody pushed him into the deep end. He barely managed to scramble to safety. Harry decided then and there that he'd better learn to swim. When he saw an ad in the newspaper offering ten free lessons at the YMCA pool, Harry jumped at the chance. In no time he was training and competing with the best swimmers in the city.

Bailey won the provincial breaststroke championships in the 50-yard, 100-yard, and 200-yard events in his teens, setting records that stood until 1943. He got into coaching when the Second World War started and the city's two regular coaches left to join the armed forces. By the time he was seventeen years old, young Harry was coaching and taking younger swimmers to meets in the Battlefords, Waskesiu, and Emma Lake. But he interrupted this career to join the navy in 1943. He put his postings to both coasts to good use, swimming in large pools whenever he had the opportunity.

Back in Saskatoon after the war, he joined "The Flying Fish," an organization of divers who performed at summer aquacades, swimming and diving entertainment performed to music. But he was still interested in coaching, and even though he was working full-time, he was instrumental in the formation of a club that would be active in winter and summer. The club was called the Y Waterbabies at first, then adopted in succession the names of the two service organizations that were its sponsors, first the Optimist, and later the Kinsmen. Ultimately, the swim club stood on its own as the Goldfins.

In later years, Bailey talked about what it was like to grow up in an era when coaching instruction was non-existent. He couldn't even find manuals or how-to books in libraries. "We read anything we could find on swimming," he reflected in a 1991 interview. "We read everything about Johnny Weissmuller [an Olympic star and one of Hollywood's great Tarzans]. I've still got a copy of *Look* magazine where it demonstrates in a series of six lessons how to do the butterfly. That's the way you learned in those days." It worked for Bailey, and the coaching techniques he perfected during those busy years worked for countless numbers of young swimmers. He combined his instinctive knowledge about technique with a quiet, low-key style. His students said they knew he meant what he said, and he never needed to raise his voice. It was said of his teaching methods that he not only encouraged the young people in his care to be good swimmers, but to be good citizens as well.

Bailey coached his students in the pool at the YMCA, and at another pool at the University of Saskatchewan, but neither was of a size that accommodated Olympic-class instruction. That pool came in 1976, when the city built the facility that was named in his honour: The Harry Bailey Aquatic Centre. The Bailey pool became one of the most popular for provincial and interprovincial swim meets, and when Saskatoon won the right to host the Canada Summer Games in the early 1990s, the pool underwent further expansion.

Products of Bailey's swimming programs excelled in world-class competitions. Among his most successful students were Martha Nelson Grant, a 1972 Olympian; Barbara Shockey-Milanese, a Pan-American Games bronze medallist who was later deprived of a shot at an Olympic medal when Canada boycotted the games in the Soviet Union in 1980; and Cheryl Hayes, four-time gold medallist at the Pan-American Games for the Deaf.

Bailey's accomplishments earned him accolades from far and wide, so it was hardly surprising that he was offered some plum coaching posts outside of Saskatchewan. But his roots were firmly in the province, and he much preferred to work with the younger swimmers. Had he accepted a job in Vancouver or Toronto, he would have been obliged to concentrate on older swimmers with their eyes on world-class competitions. In addition to his work with young people, however, he did coach Saskatchewan teams for the Canada Summer Games in 1969 and 1973, and was the Canadian coach for the Silent Swimming 13th World Games for the Deaf in Bucharest, Romania, in 1977. He was also elected president of the Saskatchewan section of the Canadian Amateur Swimming Association in 1946, and remained in that post for sixteen years.

Harry Bailey was a swimmer and coach for an incredible sixty years in Saskatchewan. He touched thousands of lives over the years, and long after he retired he was still hearing from former students. He even had letters and messages in his scrapbooks from second-generation students—competitive swimmers he had taught, just as he had taught their parents. He collected many honours. Saskatoon honoured him in 1982 with an Award of Merit and a designation as one of the top one hundred citizens of the year. He was Kinsmen Sportsman of the Year in Saskatoon in 1967, and was inducted into the Saskatchewan Sports Hall of Fame and the Canadian Aquatic Hall of Fame in 1985. He was also honoured by the community when the Harry Bailey Aquatic Centre was opened, and he was inducted into the Saskatoon Sports Hall of Fame in 1986. It was a remarkable life career for a kid with no skates, who almost drowned in a river in Tisdale.

Educator Extraordinaire

HILDA NEATBY
1904–1975

Hilda Neatby was a classroom martinet and inspiring teacher.

*N*obody seriously argues that education is not important to any progressive society, but the debate was hot and heavy fifty years ago about the controversial views expressed by Hilda Neatby, one of education's greatest advocates—also one of its most determined critics. Neatby burst upon the Saskatchewan scene publicly in 1953 with her book *So Little for the Mind*, a scathing attack on the idea of a liberal, egalitarian education— the popular theory that provided the underpinnings of public education across Canada.

Always acerbic and direct, at the time a member of the faculty of the history department at the University of Saskatchewan, Neatby challenged almost every tenet of the status quo, claiming the whole notion of egalitarianism in the classroom was folly and only served to punish the best and the brightest among the students. She accused proponents of the prevailing "pap" provided through provincial education systems of being anti-intellectual. She struck out indiscriminately at bureaucrats, curriculum writers, educators, and politicians for not questioning where the liberal education would lead.

Not surprisingly, the reaction was swift and loud. What Neatby had accomplished was to launch a debate that continues to this day. Advocates of the three-R kind of teaching, those who press for more testing, for national testing, and for rigid standards, still cite her no-holds-barred barrage of fifty years ago to bolster their cases. No doubt Neatby would be immensely gratified. She succeeded in slowing, if not stopping, the liberal education juggernaut she so despised, and she got people talking, and thinking—activities she considered to be crucial in the formation of public policy. Neatby gained a reputation across Canada as one of the most formidable intellectuals of her time, and one of the most independent thinkers. None of that came as a surprise to those who knew her well and had followed her career.

Hilda's family had immigrated to Canada from Britain when she was just two years old. Her father had been a doctor and her mother a trained musician, but their lives on a Saskatchewan homestead were typical of the times. At the same time, Hilda's mother's influence, and growing up in a household filled with books, likely encouraged Hilda to turn to intellectual pursuits at an early age. She certainly showed no interest in the rural way of life. She became a country teacher at age sixteen, and as soon as her financial situation would permit it, she enrolled at the University of Saskatchewan. Four years later, she graduated with an honours degree in history. She studied abroad for a year in Paris on a provincial government scholarship, and then returned to Saskatoon to attend Normal School (teacher training school) and complete a Master of Arts degree at the same time. She moved on and graduated with a Doctor of Philosophy in 1934 from the University of Minnesota, then returned to Saskatchewan, teaching at Regina College, a branch of the University of Saskatchewan that granted two-year arts diplomas before the University of Regina came into being in the early 1970s. She returned to Saskatoon to join the history department in 1946. She was appointed head of the department in 1958, becoming the first female head of a Canadian history department, and stayed in that post until taking early retirement in 1969. She left the University of Saskatchewan to accept a special appointment as professor of history at Queen's University in Kingston, Ontario, with specific responsibility for writing the history of that institution.

Neatby complemented her teaching career with commission work when in 1949, she was invited to become a member of the Royal Commission on National Development in the Arts, Letters and Science, known as the Massey Commission. She served for two years and was the only woman member. That commission recommended, among other things, the establishment of the Canada Council. The commission conducted a thorough and extensive investigation, immersing the members in an array of cultural issues for many months. That experience, together with the encouragement of Governor General Vincent Massey, led Neatby to write and publish *So Little for the Mind*.

She continued her teaching duties while serving on the Massey Commission, and her students, though at times fearful of her reputation, were the beneficiaries of her personal philosophies. Neatby was a martinet, but she also commanded the respect and admiration of those she taught and worked with. She was known to suffer fools badly, and had a special kind of contempt for those who abused the English language. Newspaper journalism was one of her favourite targets. She could spot a typo, a historical inaccuracy, or a violation of a rule of grammar that even the best proofreaders would miss, and she was quick to let the editors know in sharply worded letters. Neatby's pointed barbs were still being talked about when I joined the staff of the *Saskatoon StarPhoenix* in 1972.

Hilda Neatby was recognized for her work in many ways during a long and productive career. She was granted honorary degrees from Brock University, the University of Toronto, the University of Windsor, and the University of Saskatchewan. She was named citizen of the year in Saskatoon in 1954; she had a Fellowship in the Royal Society of Canada; and was among the first to be invested as a Companion of the Order of Canada in 1967.

Neatby was one of this country's earliest feminists, writing and speaking often about the role of women in the professions, and in society in general. Though she was best known for her book criticizing the education system, she also wrote other books and innumerable academic papers. In her last book, *And Not to Yield*, she wrote passionately about religion, history, politics, and the role of women. She concluded, rather sadly, that she had learned that Canada was not ready for an "uncompromising intellectual woman reformer," as she had to expend too much of her energy just holding firm instead of going forward with the reforms she believed in. Her elitism showed in the book, but her appeals were clear:

I want to urge only that educational and societal aims need not be such a clutter of nice things flung by well-meaning people into a sort of democratic catch-all. We should seek rather a simple and profound expression of the truths by which men have always lived; truths which may be abundantly developed and enriched by our imaginations and our endeavors but which must not be smothered in professional jargon.

Hilda Neatby, lover of language, tireless and passionate about education, did indeed leave her mark, despite her opinion that Canada was not ready for her.

Books for the Regions

MARION GILROY

1912–1981

Marion Gilroy took on the daunting task of organizing
the province's first regional library.

*O*ne of the individuals to whom the Saskatchewan of today owes a great debt of gratitude is often referred to as "the small woman in the big hat driving the big black van." Her name was Marion Gilroy, and her accomplishments are nothing short of heroic. Gilroy came to the province when its people were going through one of the biggest struggles of their lives to recover from years of depression, followed by years of service in an overseas war. She convinced large numbers of farmers and rural council members to support her drive to create regional libraries. Only someone who grew up in that era can fully comprehend the challenges she faced, and the improvements she made to the lives of thousands.

Libraries were a tough sell to people who, just a few years earlier, barely had enough to eat. The notion of "food for the soul," of the sort books could provide, was not accorded a high priority by people who lived by hard labour and were often culturally disposed to mistrust the things that came out of books, let alone the people who read books. It was a struggle to keep schools open in many areas. Many farm fathers scoffed at the idea that their sons would benefit from anything more than the most basic schooling. Many would argue that educating daughters who would just marry neighbour boys and raise children was a waste of money.

For someone like Gilroy, who had three degrees and had grown up in a household where books and reading were held in high esteem, approaching and convincing people that libraries were needed was a daunting task. But she was resourceful and determined. More importantly, Marion Gilroy understood that she was not dealing with bad people, but people who lived hard lives and to whom practical considerations were matters of life and death. She was neither condescending nor dismissive of their genuine concerns, but she was committed to her cause, and it showed.

Gilroy came to Saskatchewan in November of 1946. Born in Springhill, Nova Scotia, in 1912, she had spent most of her life in the Maritimes. She held a Bachelor of Arts degree from Acadia University, a Library Science degree from Columbia University in New York, and a Master of Arts from the University of Toronto. She had an extensive resume covering her work as an archivist, researcher, and librarian and was convinced to move to the west to head a program to bring regional libraries to rural areas. She came highly recommended, but must have had some serious doubts after getting off the train to be greeted by an early blizzard and plummeting temperatures. She had the title of Supervisor of Regional Libraries, a tiny office, a car, and a modest budget, but little idea of how to proceed. And to make matters worse, even though she had been promised a house or apartment, Regina was experiencing a severe post-war housing shortage. There was no accommodation to be had. She started her life in the province as houseguest of the provincial librarian, Mrs. Austin Bothwell.

Although Gilroy had the authority of a newly minted piece of legislation, the Regional Library Act 1946, passed by the equally new CCF government, the mandate still left a lot to her own initiative. The province, to its credit, had squeezed out enough to put what amounted to seed money into regional library programs, but it was still up to local governments to pay half the cost of their libraries. This was a significant obstacle.

The idea of regional libraries—of serving the various regions of the province with something similar to the libraries already established in the major urban centres—enjoyed some solid support. Many women's groups backed the libraries, as did most teachers. Some school board officials were supportive, but by no means all of them. The clergy, the RCMP, and a scattering of high-profile individuals, especially people associated with the University of Saskatchewan, were all on side. But at the outset, no councils from smaller centres approved of the plan. Any that leaned in that direction quickly changed their minds when they found out that they'd have to raise taxes to finance regional libraries. In addition, the Tommy Douglas CCF government still had its enemies in rural Saskatchewan, and some were not above using the library program to push their political views. One story that persisted was that the libraries would be used to indoctrinate young people in the ways of socialism.

But Gilroy was undeterred. She quickly took stock and realized that her first task would be to survey the province, then begin her work by finding one area of focus. It was one of the worst winters Saskatchewan had seen for years. The road system back then left much to be desired, but Gilroy still undertook a rigorous schedule of travel. She was turning up in centres across the province, giving talks, listening to responses, and looking for that ideal situation. She had more than one close call that winter as she plied the highways with the new Ford car the government provided, but she managed to get through the winter with no serious problems. She also became convinced that the area where she would secure that all-important first regional setup was in the northwest of the province, with Prince Albert as the central point.

The Prince Albert area seemed to be right, but not because the regional library idea had been warmly received outside the city of Prince Albert. In fact, Gilroy had started out with a solid wall of rejection. But the area had the right demographics—she needed about twenty-five thousand people—and it had another big advantage, a mayor in Prince Albert who was well known, popular, and a strong supporter of the library. The mayor, John Cuelenaere, did indeed prove to be most helpful, as did an ad hoc committee that included Betty Davis, the wife of the editor of the *Prince Albert Daily Herald*, and Marion Sherman, a long-time member of the Prince Albert Council. The three were staunch allies of Gilroy for the next three years, the time it took to convince enough rural municipal governments to get on side and make it possible to declare the North Central Saskatchewan Regional Library a reality.

It was a tough struggle. The government was getting impatient, cutting Gilroy's already measly budget in order to appease a niggling opposition. A school principal from one of the small towns in the area took up the cry that a regional library would just be a tool for CCF propaganda. When such enemies of the CCF tried to capitalize on scaremongering, Gilroy just carried on with her voice of reason, and she prevailed. Always, the problem of a tax levy to run a library came up as the most formidable obstacle.

Marion Gilroy became a familiar figure around Prince Albert. She travelled the back roads, pressing her case relentlessly. She had a sound argument and a well-prepared presentation that included a film on distribution of books to outlying areas. She appealed to book lovers wherever she found them, and she appealed to reason in others. She was never combative, though she certainly had more than enough provocation.

When the North Central Region, now known as the Wapiti Regional Library, was finally in operation, Gilroy put a capable librarian in charge and turned her attention to the rest of the province. Over the next thirteen years she laid the groundwork for two more regional libraries, and then accepted a position as a member of the faculty of the School of Library Science at the University of British Columbia, where she passed on her dream of a dynamic library service to another generation.

Saskatchewan Teachers' Federation

Giant in Public Eduction

STIRLING MCDOWELL

1931–2000

Stirling McDowell outside the Saskatchewan Teachers' Federation building in
Saskatoon at the time of his retirement as STF General Secretary in 1982.

Those close to Stirling McDowell spoke of him as a modest man who made an immense impact on the teaching profession in Saskatchewan. As general secretary of the large and politically powerful Saskatchewan Teachers' Federation (STF), he left his mark on curricula, on the system of negotiating teachers' contracts, and on relationships between teachers, school boards, and the provincial Department of Education. Furthermore, Stirling McDowell was able to insert himself into the middle of the charged atmosphere traditionally existing between the three pillars of the education establishment in the province—trustees, politicians, and teachers—and bring an aura of calm and common sense to bear.

No one would describe Stirling McDowell as a charismatic leader. He was indeed a modest man, but the results of his quiet style certainly rivalled those achieved by more flamboyant or combative individuals. Somehow, he earned the respect of the school trustees who had to levy the taxes to pay teachers, the politicians and bureaucrats who did the bargaining, and the teachers he represented. And he didn't do it by compromising the interests of any of the teachers he spoke for. As a former teacher, McDowell knew very well the difficulties faced by those at the bottom of the pile, and just how long it took for the system to recognize their real worth. He was also well aware that inequalities of the past between established teachers and newcomers and the failure of the system to address the problem had contributed substantially to a teacher shortage in Saskatchewan. The incentives Saskatchewan provided to young teachers when McDowell was general secretary in 1967 just weren't good enough to keep them there. The profession made steady gains in wages and benefits during his tenure as head of the STF, while McDowell and others worked toward rebalancing remuneration between the highest and the lowest on the pay scale.

The 1931 Saskatchewan into which Stirling McDowell was born had little compassion and few developed resources. Agriculture was the mainstay of the still-young province. With the double whammy of the stock market crash of 1929 and the ensuing economic depression, followed by the onset of a long period of drought, farmers were struggling as never before. Because McDowell grew up in the province, he fully appreciated the nature of the economy that had to support two important services: the public education system, which shares prominence with the other "jewel in the crown," health care. Generations of Saskatchewan people continue to place a high value on both. Together, they have formed the centrepiece of a public policy that reveals compassion for the less fortunate, and an egalitarian approach to sharing wealth generated by publicly owned resources.

The senior McDowell had moved to Saskatchewan from Ontario in 1908, homesteading in the McCord area in the south. The southern part of the province was the centre of the dustbowl when the Dirty Thirties started, so he had moved north to Nipawin, where the family was living when Stirling was born. They returned to McCord after the Depression, but in later years Stirling would recall that farm life was still very difficult. Like thousands of others in post-Depression, post-war Saskatchewan, young Stirling looked for a different way to make a living. He was taking his last year of grade twelve at Central Collegiate in Regina when a biology teacher started him as a lab assistant. That got him interested in the teaching profession. He attended Normal School in Saskatoon for a year, taught for three years in Outlook, and then was able to enroll in the University of Saskatchewan. There, he obtained a Bachelor of Education degree in 1955, and a Bachelor of Arts degree in 1956. He taught for one year at the Rosetown Composite High School, then joined the staff of the Saskatchewan Teachers' Federation. He earned a Master of Education degree at the University of Saskatchewan in 1963, followed by a Doctor of Philosophy in educational administration from the University of Alberta in 1965.

During the 1950s and early 1960s, Stirling McDowell was also rising through the ranks in the STF, working first as an executive assistant, then as assistant general secretary, and finally, in 1967, as general secretary. He held that position for fifteen busy, productive years. Teacher qualifications improved during that time; as well, demands grew for salary increases. McDowell once referred to the years of "creative tensions," caused by the unilateral bargaining system in use at the time—a system Stirling helped change to bi-level bargaining. That returned some autonomy to local boards, while leaving the salary issue to be settled by government bargainers.

Because of his successes at the STF, all political parties pursued McDowell to go into partisan politics, and the public service frequently tried to recruit him for deputy minister of the education department. But he steadfastly refused all offers, content to work toward the goals he had set as head of the STF. McDowell headed the STF under both Liberal and NDP (New Democratic Party) governments. Both Liberal premier Ross Thatcher and NDP premier Allan Blakeney acknowledged the role teachers had played in the stunning defeat of the Liberals in 1971. In the ensuing years, McDowell built on that teacher power, while building a new level of co-operation between the province's various educational agencies.

After retiring from the STF in 1982, Stirling McDowell was appointed secretary general of the Canadian Teachers' Federation. Over the next ten years in that position, he worked internationally to export the Saskatchewan teacher's experience to other nations and to other educational systems. Again McDowell was lauded for his skill as a negotiator and his ability to encourage co-operation between educational agencies. And his public service wasn't just limited to the educational arena. After retiring from his position with the Canadian Teachers' Federation, McDowell accepted the chairmanship of a committee on compensation for MLAs in Saskatchewan. Among other things, McDowell's report resulted in Saskatchewan becoming only the second province in Canada to fully tax MLAs' salaries. In 1997, Stirling McDowell received the Saskatchewan Order of Merit, the most prestigious award the province confers—a highly fitting tribute to a man who devoted his life to improving education, at home and abroad.

Sailing the Prairie

TOM SUKANEN

1878 – 1943

Tom Sukanen, the man who built an ocean-going vessel on his prairie farm.

It's a tourist attraction in southern Saskatchewan now, and a popular one by all accounts, but the ocean-going ship *Sontiainen* is also a symbol. It's one that is recognized by those who are old enough to remember the dark days of the Great Depression and the need felt by so many to escape the relentless wind, the choking dust, and the spectre of so many dreams turned into nightmares. To its builder, the obsessed Finnish immigrant Tom Sukanen, the *Sontiainen* symbolized the success he achieved in his new land; concrete evidence of his hard work, in which he could actually sail home to Finland to show his family. He made an elaborate plan and executed it with near perfection, but we'll never know whether it would have worked. All we do know is that Sukanen destroyed himself and his dream. He became an object of ridicule, with his life's work a target for vandals. Ostracized by a whole community because he did not conform, he ended his days in a psychiatric ward far from home and family.

It wasn't always like that. Tom Sukanen was once widely admired for his strength and his capability. He could make things with his hands, and he once amassed the tidy sum of $9,000 through frugal living and good farming practices on his homestead in the Macrorie area, just a bit northwest of Outlook. He was a loner, but a good neighbour—a man known for his dry sense of humour and generosity with his time and talents. He believed in self-sufficiency. He once built a threshing machine and harvested his own crop and the crops of several neighbours. He built a sewing machine, and it worked so well that the women of the community often borrowed it to sew clothes for their children. He knitted a suit for himself out of binder twine, and it was widely admired for fit and style. He even built a tricycle that neighbourhood children loved to ride.

Born Tomi Jannus Alankola in Finland in September 1878, by age twenty Tom stood 1.8 metres tall and weighed over 90 kilograms. He was trained as a shipbuilder and steelworker. Tomi had already gained extensive experience at sailing and navigating when he decided to join his older brother, who had come to Canada to try his hand at farming. Instead, Tomi ended up in Minnesota, where he started farming. For reasons no longer known, Tomi's last name was changed to Sukanen, and he dropped the "i" from his first name, perhaps thinking he would fit in better in his adopted land. He met and married a young Finnish woman who was trying to carry on the farm left by her dead father, and they tried to make a success of things together. But times were tough. The two had three children, but their farm was failing. Tom decided to head north to Canada to see if he could do better on a homestead near his brother. His plan was to file claim on a homestead, get established, and bring his family to join him.

He walked the 960 kilometres or so, living off the land and navigating by the stars. He filed a claim on land about 16 kilometres from his brother's farm, and set about making a new life. By 1918, with money in the bank and a successful farming operation established, he headed back to Minnesota to get his family, again on foot. When Tom arrived, he found no one. His wife had died in a flu epidemic; his children had been dispatched to foster homes. After a long search he found one child, a son, and took him away, intending to take him back to Canada, but the American authorities intervened and took the child back to the foster home. Tom tried again, but was threatened with jail and deported. He never saw any of his children again.

Back on his farm, Tom became something of a recluse. He kept the farm up though, and worked on a rail gang for a while. In 1929, he decided to return to Finland for a visit, travelling up the Saskatchewan River in a rowboat he built himself. He reached Hudson Bay, where he got a job on a freighter and worked his passage to Finland. He was back in Canada within a month. It appears that the trip may have been the precursor to his scheme to return to his homeland in an ocean-going vessel he would build right there on his farm. He obtained a complete set of maps from the archives in Regina. Not long after his return, big loads of steel and lumber began to arrive.

Among his papers found years later, was the blueprint for the vessel Tom designed. It was 13 metres long and 8.5 metres high, to be built in three sections. It was highly sophisticated and, according to engineers who examined the papers, quite capable of an ocean voyage. The plan was for the keel and hull to be watertight, so they could be floated in shallow water. The finished vessel would be steam powered or it could travel under sail. The cabins would be loaded onto a large raft, which would be powered by motor and have a rudder. Tom was going to maneuver the two sections up the Saskatchewan River at its peak flow, reach the deep water of the Nelson, and then on to Hudson Bay. There he would complete the building by putting the three parts together and installing the steam engine, then launch the craft and make for Greenland, then Iceland, and finally to Finland.

As the already reclusive Tom Sukanen set to work forging parts by hand and assembling the skeleton of the craft, he became less and less communicative. Neighbours could hear him, day after day and late into the night, hammering on his forge, with the hot coals sending up sparks and a red glow. He grew thinner and more haggard every day, but the work went on. The years of the Depression went by, but it seemed Tom barely noticed, so obsessed was he with his task. To the community, his project became "that crazy ship," and Tom "the crazy Finn." But the ship was taking shape. Tom named her the *Sontiainen*, the Finnish word for water beetle, an insect he much admired for its skill in the water. By 1941, with his money gone and little or no food left, he was able to transport the boat cabins the twenty-seven kilometres to the water's edge. But when he asked a neighbour if he could use his steam engine to tow the keel and hull to the water, the man angrily refused. Then vandals struck the boat cabins, smashing much of what Tom had accomplished.

The acts of vandalism on his work seemed to mark a turning

point of sorts for Tom. Even members of his brother's family could barely recognize him. He refused all offers of food and did not want to see anyone. Thin as a rail and blackened from the smoke of the forge, he was a strange and frightening figure. Soon a group of neighbours called in the RCMP. After much deliberation, a somewhat questionable charge was laid against Tom Sukanen of obstructing a waterway. Ultimately, it led to Tom's incarceration in the psychiatric hospital in North Battleford, where he died in deep depression in 1943. He remained silent and morose, though he did ask one of his few remaining friends to protect his ship until his return.

The *Sontiainen* lay in pieces in a farmer's field for thirty years, until a group led by Laurence "Moon" Mullen, a Moose Jaw area farmer, had the pieces hauled to a pioneer village in a field in southern Saskatchewan and started a project to reconstruct the ship. After years of fundraising and volunteer effort, they were able to hold a grand opening of an exhibit featuring the infamous craft in 1977. The name had been changed to "*Dontiainen*," apparently because the original paint had faded so badly that a mistake was made, but the ship was restored to plan. Among other things, the group had arranged to move Tom Sukanen's remains to be reburied in a plot beside the ship.

A single white cross marks the spot, with a bronze plaque bearing the words "Tom Sukanen, Shipbuilder." Years later, well into his nineties, Mullen told a reporter that he had taken up the cause of restoring the ship to honour Sukanen's memory. "Tom Sukanen didn't do anything wrong," Mullen is quoted as saying. "He wasn't crazy. He just wanted to go home."

Master of Many Talents

NORMAN WARD

1918–1990

Norman Ward watching the results come in
during the federal election of 1963.

"The only ambition I ever had was to be a singer," said Norman Ward of his eclectic life. He once told an interviewer that his life and his successes were the result of a series of happy accidents. While his real ambition was to become an opera singer (which he never did), Ward's avocation was writing; his profession was educator. Norman Ward was also living proof that you could be a credible political scientist and a humour writer at the same time.

The first time I saw Norman Ward, he was working as a television commentator on a provincial election broadcast. I was working in Alberta at the time and visiting my parents, who were very interested in the outcome of what had been a typically acrimonious election campaign in Saskatchewan. While interested in the election, I was also curious about Ward. My brother-in-law had lent me a copy of Ward's 1960 book *Mice in the Beer*, a satirical and subtle volume which I had enjoyed. The notion of a published humourist who was also an authority on provincial politics intrigued me.

Television was in its infancy in the province at the time. A private Saskatoon television station was the only one available—"snow" on the screen and all—on my parents' farm at Kindersley. The station had recruited several "talking heads" to fill the long stretches between announcements of progress in the vote counting. Of the five men sitting around a table in the studio, two were terrified of the camera, two others were too fond of the sound of their own voices when they had nothing to say, and one, Norman Ward, was relaxed, erudite, and, at times, given to funny little asides. It was the first of many times I watched him over the years performing the same task after federal, provincial, and even municipal elections. For Ward, the twin pursuits of political science and humour writing seemed to complement each other quite nicely.

In fact, Ward had been a writer long before he became a professor of political science, and before he even heard of the University of Saskatchewan, where he would end up having a long and successful career. He liked to tell the story of how he won a writing contest in a British magazine when he was still in public school. The prize was a whopping sixty cents, and it was paid in stamps. He had to talk his father into buying the stamps from him before he could actually enjoy his meagre reward.

Truly a man of many parts, Norman Ward was content with his lot as husband, father of six, and one of the most respected scholars in the country on the topic of Canadian politics. A distinguished and popular professor at the University of Saskatchewan, Ward became a faculty member in 1945. He was elected a Fellow of the Royal Society in 1962, and appointed Britnell Professor in the Department of Economics and Political Science in 1969—a professorship in memory of Dr. G. E. Britnell, head of the department from 1945–1961. Ward was also invested as an Officer of the Order of Canada in 1974. He contributed in practical ways to the political life of the province too, serving in 1965–66 as vice-chairman of the Electoral Boundaries Commission for Saskatchewan, and working as a member of the Federal Advisory Committee on Elections Expenses.

Born in Hamilton, Ontario, Norman Ward attended the local McMaster University. He reckoned in later years that if the university hadn't moved to Hamilton from Toronto he would never have been able to attend. It was only because he could live at home that he could afford a university education. He studied economics merely because the boy next door was taking the same course; Norman knew little or nothing about the subject and had even less interest in it. Then the Second World War broke out and one of his professors enlisted; the one that was left taught political science. That was a subject that did interest Ward, and in due course he did his thesis on a political subject.

In a somewhat similar pattern, Norman and his new wife Betty "stumbled" onto Saskatchewan in 1945 after spending a year in the Maritimes. All they knew for sure was that they didn't want to go back to southern Ontario, so they took a closer look when a job opened up at the University of Saskatchewan. Ward recalls being impressed by finding "the political laboratory of the whole world" there, with the CCF just taking over and changes sweeping the province. Saskatchewan was the place to be for a political scientist.

The Wards also loved the life and pace of a small city with no traffic jams, safe streets, and clean air. And Norman could work at his writing, which he did in his own inimitable fashion, sitting in his living room with a board over the arms of his chair and his research material in piles beside him on the floor. The noise and turmoil of several small children and one active dog would swirl, while he worked on, oblivious. *Mice in the Beer* earned him the Stephen Leacock Medal for Humour. That was followed in 1964 with *The Fully Processed Cheese*, and then in 1977 with *Her Majesty's Mice*. The books were all short story collections, crafted in Ward's special essaylike style, not the kind of humour that brings big guffaws, but rather the subtle variety with irony and unique little twists.

As well, Ward turned out a steady stream of academic papers, along with several books on Canadian politics. The national political scene was what interested him, and it was his contention that the best view of Ottawa was gained by living elsewhere and looking in—rather than being up close, inside the never-ending boil and bubble of political life. He wrote *The Canadian House of Commons: Representation* (1950), *Government in Canada* (1960), and *The Public Purse: A Study in Canadian Democracy* (1962). He co-edited *Politics in Saskatchewan* and edited *A Party Politician: the Memoirs of Chubby Power*, and *The Politician* by James G. (Jimmy) Gardiner, who was twice premier of Saskatchewan and served as federal agriculture minister.

As he wrote, he also taught. Ward's classes were always popular with University of Saskatchewan students. Stories abound about his classroom humour, but he once reminded a student that it was his serious persona that set exams and did the grading. One of the stories has it that when he was just starting out in the department, a student asked him how long his essay should be. The young professor responded that he intended to grade the papers by throwing them down a flight of stairs and awarding the highest mark to the one closest to the top, since it would be the lightest of the lot. Gravity would send the weightier papers to the bottom, he said.

Ward took the writing part of his life very seriously. He valued his associations with other writers and was well known in prairie writing circles, serving a term as chairman of the board of the Saskatchewan Writers Guild, and appearing as a banquet speaker at the Guild's 1972 Fall Conference and Annual General Meeting. He also conducted workshops on humour and historical writing.

All his life, Ward took great delight in poking a stick in the eye of the pompous establishment. And it seemed that the person he took least seriously of all was himself. Norman Ward summed up his life in his own way, in a biography he provided for inclusion in his book *Mice in the Beer*.

At various times I have been a soda jerk, a production chaser in a wire mill, a secretary to a royal commission, a cartoonist's gag-writer, a journalist, a chairman of countless boards of conciliation in labour-management disputes and a holder of all academic ranks from tutorial assistant to professor. I never actually wanted to be any of those things — the only ambition I ever had was to be a singer and when you consider that many of the things I have done involved a lot of work, while nowadays it takes neither talent nor experience to be a singer, there are times when I wonder how I got off the track. Part of the trouble, of course, is that I was born so lazy that I am ashamed of it and I have been working like a dog since early youth to keep people from finding out about it.

In 1969, Ward was designated biographer for the twice-premier of Saskatchewan, Jimmy Gardiner. This work was Ward's last major undertaking. When illness intervened, Norman asked his long-time friend and associate, David Smith, to complete the book. They share the byline on *Jimmy Gardiner: Relentless Liberal*, an authoritative volume that came out in 1990, the same year Norman Ward died.

Man of Peace

PETER MAKAROFF

1894 – 1970

Crusading lawyer Peter Makaroff, seated
centre front, with fellow Doukhobors.

eter Makaroff was a man of principle who fought for the things he believed, in ways he believed—the ways of reasoned debate and peaceful protest. Unmoved by fickle public opinion, Makaroff persisted in steadfastly sticking up for those who were persecuted or prosecuted for their political beliefs. Described by one admirer as "a noted Canadian peacemaker, lawyer and humanitarian," Peter George Makaroff made his mark in Saskatchewan legal circles and beyond.

In one of his most famous cases, Makaroff, with the help of sometime courtroom foe Emmett Hall, defended the trekkers who were accused of starting a riot in Regina in the summer of 1935. Ostracized by most of the Saskatchewan legal community, Makaroff and Hall believed that the men deserved a proper defence. They were not convinced that the police were totally innocent in the events that led up to the night of violence on the streets of the prairie city. Makaroff and Hall didn't keep all of their clients out of jail, but they assured that sentences meted out to those convicted were, by most accounts, not excessive.

Peter Makaroff was born in Russia, into a family that was part of a religious sect known as Doukhobors, or spirit wrestlers. A community of illiterate peasants, for the most part, the Doukhobors opposed war and resisted military conscription. Not surprisingly, they were *persona non grata* in Czarist Russia. Their plight came to the attention of the Quakers of North America, and they were able to negotiate an acceptable emigration arrangement, under which a large group of Doukhobors came to western Canada to become pioneer farmers in colonies on the prairies. The Makaroffs were part of that group. They settled in colonies. Makaroff's colony settled on the banks of the South Saskatchewan River in 1899 in what would become the Blaine Lake district.

Peter grew up experiencing the religious and economic freedom the Doukhobors had been promised. He became devoted at an early age to the preservation of that freedom. Young Peter came to the attention of the Society of Friends, the Quaker group that had helped his family and others escape persecution in Russia. They helped him receive a quality education. Peter finished his schooling at the Rosthern Academy, and by age sixteen was working as a school teacher. He saved his money and enrolled in the newly minted University of Saskatchewan, obtaining a Bachelor of Arts in 1915, and Bachelor of Law in 1918—the first non-Anglo-Saxon student to get a law degree at the university. Indeed, it was claimed by some that he was the first Doukhobor in the world to record such an achievement.

Makaroff opened his own law practice in Saskatoon in 1918. After his first law partner died, Roger and Mary Carter joined the practice. Peter's reputation grew, and in 1932 he was made a Queen's Counsel. One of his most high profile cases was his defence of Peter Veregin Jr. The junior Veregin had been recruited to come to Canada from Russia to lead the Doukhobors, after his father was assassinated. Peter Veregin Sr. had been known as "the king of the Doukhobors" in Canada. After his father's assassination, Peter Veregin Jr. broke with tradition and organized the radical Sons of Freedom, a group whose goals Peter Makaroff did not share. But when the Canadian government threatened to deport the firebrand Veregin, Makaroff stepped in. In order to reach his client before he was spirited out of the country from Halifax, the lawyer had to catch a ride on a small aircraft, riding in an open-air cockpit across the Bay of Fundy from Boston to Halifax. He made it in time and the deportation was stopped, but it was by no means the end of Veregin's need for legal counsel. As the Sons of Freedom battled the British Columbia and federal governments over compulsory education, their leader, Veregin, was often in trouble—and in court. Makaroff did not let personal differences deny the leader a legal defence.

But headline-grabbing courtroom cases weren't all Peter Makaroff was about. He worked tirelessly for social justice, first as a member of the Progressive Party in Saskatchewan, and then as part of the new farmer–labour alliance that brought unions and other labour organizations together with farmers in the search for better lives for all. That movement became the CCF. Makaroff was a close friend of CCF founder J. S. Woodsworth. The two shared a vision of social justice and world peace, and they also believed in the original aims of the CCF, among them affordable and accessible health care for all, and an end to the poverty of many prairie families. Makaroff was also well known for his unsympathetic views on the world of big business, one of the CCF's favourite targets. A man known for his dry wit as well as his courageous courtroom stands, years later Makaroff liked to tell the story of how he drew the anger of the judge in the trial of the trekkers in Regina by observing that there was a close parallel between "a peaceful assembly of trekkers … and a business meeting of a board of bank directors."

That early political activity did not translate into electoral success for Makaroff, however. He ran first in the Saskatchewan election of 1934 in the constituency of Shellbrook, and then in federal elections in 1940 and 1948 in the Rosthern riding, but was turned down by voters each time. He did, however, win election to Saskatoon City Council, serving one term, 1939–40. He also served on the University of Saskatchewan Board of Governors in 1945, and was chairman of the Saskatchewan Labour Relations Board from the early 1950s to 1964. Above all, however, he was known best for his work for world peace.

Peter Makaroff served as chairman of the Saskatchewan Branch of the World Federalists, and shortly before his death established the World Federalist Prize to finance a yearly award for the best essay relating to world peace through world law. In the 1960s, he joined a group of peacemakers in protesting chemical, biological, and radiological warfare tests at the Suffield, Alberta, Defence Research Station. In November of that year he took part, along with four hundred others, in a meeting at the gates of the radar base at Orcadia, Saskatchewan, to discuss non-violent action, one world, peace, and universal brotherhood. The following year he was part of a fifteen-hundred–strong peace vigil in the rain at the RCAF radar base at Dana, Saskatchewan, where the gathering presented a strongly worded statement to the base commander, expressing grave concern for the survival of the human race. A year later, Peter Makaroff was at the podium addressing the International Meeting for Peace held at the Peace Gardens on the Manitoba–North Dakota border, followed by attendance in Ottawa at the 14th World Congress of the Association of World Federalists.

Peter Makaroff did not seek personal fame or acclaim in his life. He asked that no eulogies be given after his death, and that his passing not be marked in any way. In all probability he would have preferred to be remembered by the words of one of the statements he helped to write in support of the anti-war cause he so passionately pursued:

> We meet ... to manifest our grave concern for the survival of the human race. Man's traditional reliance on war for security now threatens us with extinction ... Man is the measure. Craving life for our children and bearing no malice toward any men's children, we present ourselves as petition to the world's leaders to take immediate steps toward the prevention of universal suicide.

Such was the dedication and passion toward world peace of Peter Makaroff, Doukhobor immigrant, son of Saskatchewan, man of principle, man of peace.

The Queen of Hearts

SANDRA SCHMIRLER

1963–2000

Sandra Schmirler was a gold-medal Olympic curler.

*A*ll too often it is the brightest star that fades the fastest. That certainly could be said of Sandra Schmirler, Saskatchewan's, and Canada's, diva and Olympic star in the Canadian prairies game of curling. Schmirler's death from cancer at an untimely age not only cut short a brilliant sports career, but also ended the life of a woman who was loved and highly regarded both on and off the ice. Indeed, when two national networks gave full coverage of her funeral in Regina in 2000, it was said that the audience numbers far exceeded that of any funeral ever held for a sports figure in this country. Schmirler connected with people across the country, including thousands who were not the kind of curling fans she grew up with in her hometown of Biggar. Those who knew Sandra Schmirler ruefully observed that she would probably have asked in all sincerity, what all the fuss was about. When a writer once approached Sandra about doing a book on her life, she responded with genuine surprise, "Oh, do you really think anybody cares?"

In truth, many sports figures are best revered from a distance. Qualities important on the playing field don't always make the nicest human beings. Sandra Schmirler had all the instincts that make a winner in the highly competitive sport of curling. However, she left all the sharp edges on the ice. That seemed to be the key to her immense popularity, long before she became ill. Placing the element of self-interest above all else seems to have a lot to do with a "winning" attitude in competitive sport. This attitude appears to have simply passed Sandra Schmirler by. In her private life, Sandra was a compassionate friend, with a keen interest in the world around her.

Sandra Schmirler had a rather ordinary upbringing in an ordinary Saskatchewan town, with family and friends around her, and no great designs on fame and fortune. She was the youngest of three daughters born to Art and Shirley Schmirler. The couple had moved to Biggar in the 1950s. Art worked for the railroad, Shirley for the local hospital as a nursing aide. Sandra took her schooling in Biggar and, like so many others, did some curling in the winter. But Sandra demonstrated early on that she was an above average shot maker and ultimately ended up, while still a teenager, playing with a couple of adult rinks before she moved to Saskatoon to attend the University of Saskatchewan. After obtaining a degree in physical education, she found a job working in the City of Regina's leisure services department. And Sandra kept curling.

Gradually, "Schmirler the curler," as she was nicknamed by a fellow worker, made a name for herself. As she rose through the various levels of competition, she played with a series of different teams and met the women who were increasingly bringing their game into the public eye. In a province like Saskatchewan, many liken curling to a religion. Skilful play gets noticed. And when one of the top teams in the province went looking for help to reach the finals, it was natural for them to seek out Sandra Schmirler. She came through, and the team made it to the nationals.

Among the players Sandra met, and seemed to mesh with, were the three who would eventually accompany her to the very pinnacle of curling, an Olympic gold medal. They were Jan Betker, Joan McCusker, and Marcia Gudereit. After a few years of playing with—once in a while playing against—each other, the three got together to form their own team or rink, with Sandra as skip, Jan third, Joan second, and Marcia lead. It was kismet. The four played the game with an intensity that set new standards in women's curling, but they also had fun. And they were fun to watch. In the years 1993 to 1998 when they were winning first a provincial title, then a national, and finally a world crown, television was discovering a sizeable audience for a sport that had once been thought far too slow to make good TV. The Schmirler rink (though it was Peterson for a time after Sandra's first marriage) brought a new excitement to curling. Sandra had a habit of winning games with her last curling rock, or relying on her ability to pull off spectacular shots that got spectators involved. And when it came time for the inevitable post-game interviews, it didn't hurt that Sandra was pretty, vivacious, and extremely articulate.

The 1990s were busy and productive, for the most part, though Sandra went through some personal trials. Her marriage failed, and the breakup and divorce shook her badly. But with the support of her teammates, who were by then also her closest friends, she was soon back on track. And it was some track. The Schmirler rink was virtually unbeatable for several seasons. They captured a record three-time win of the national Scott Tournament of Hearts competitions (thus Sandra's Queen of Hearts nickname), and went on to win three times in world championship competitions. Sandra was on top of her game by 1998 and dealing with unprecedented celebrity. She carried it off with poise and class, cementing her relationship with appreciative fans who remained loyal to her for as long as she curled.

Sandra met and married a man named Shannon English in 1996. Unlike her first husband, Shannon strongly supported her goals in curling. And she and her teammates had their eyes on another challenge. After years of indecision and demonstrations, the Olympic Committee had decided to make curling an official sport of the Winter Olympics for the 1998 games. The Schmirler rink had previously competed to be the demonstration team, but had missed in the final. They wouldn't make the same mistake with a gold medal at stake. In one of her classic nail-biting finishes, Sandra took her team through the toughest competition of its life and came out on top. The Schmirler curling rink from Biggar, Saskatchewan, was off to represent Canada in the Olympics!

Again, Sandra had some personal issues to deal with. She and Shannon had both wanted children, and she had given birth to their first child, a little girl they named Sarah, just months before the Nagano Olympic Games. She left for Japan in tears, very reluctant to leave Sarah at that tender age. She knew the child was safe and sound with relatives, but she was still devastated. But again she rose to the occasion. As all of Canada watched, the rink of Sandra, Jan, Joan, and Marcia rolled through the round robin part of the week, undefeated. Then in the semi-final against Britain, they had a close call, but won, with the help of some of Sandra's patented last rock magic. They then went on to defeat the Danes in a final that had its moments of panic, but was under Canadian control for the most part. The Schmirler rink had won the gold. Canadians were ecstatic.

Not surprisingly, Sandra and her teammates were exhausted, but they only had a few days before their next competition. As third-time winners of the Scott Tournament of Hearts the previous year, they were automatically in the national finals for 1998. The tournament was in Regina, and Sandra and her team were headliners. They gave a valiant effort, but given their circumstances, they just didn't have what it took. They bowed out before the playoffs.

Sandra was dabbling a bit in sports broadcasting and pregnant with her second child when she began to experience the pain in her back. Little did she know then that this heralded the onset of a virulent cancer that took her life, two years, almost to the day, after her great triumph at Nagano.

Lavish tributes came from people across the country who Sandra had touched during her short and brilliant career. Many were new fans, and others, like those in my household, had watched her progress for years. We still watch women's curling and probably in our minds compare the up-and-coming skips who march across our screen to that one true champion we still miss. It's not the same without her.

Diefenbaker Canada Centre Archives MG01/XVII/JGD 6480

The Museum Man

GEORGE SHEPHERD
1890–1978

George Shepherd, named curator of the Western Development Museum in
Saskatoon in 1953, pictured at the museum with Queen Elizabeth and
Prince Philip during the Royal visit of 1959.

*S*askatchewan owes a large debt of gratitude to the people who came here and turned a raw frontier into the resource-rich province it became, as well as to those who had the foresight to preserve the history of those frontier days. George Shepherd did both, leaving a legacy as farmer, rancher, museum curator, and staunch supporter of all efforts to keep our history intact.

Shepherd was born in 1890 in a small town in the county of Kent, known as the garden spot of England. He was the second in a family of six sons and one daughter. His father was a butcher, his mother a homemaker. The shop was in the front of the house and the animals—whose parts were later set out for sale—had to be driven through a passageway in the Shepherd's living quarters to the slaughter area in the back yard. Eventually, the family moved the small business to a coastal town in search of more profits. Again the shop was part of the house, but the slaughtering was done two blocks away. Unfortunately, the hoped-for profits didn't materialize, and the Shepherds decided to answer the call for settlers on the Great Plains of the British colony of Canada.

It was a bold move. They knew little of farming—indeed Shepherd senior had tried it once and failed. The Shepherds knew even less of Canada. But the lure of free land was strong, and the adventure was an attractive prospect for George, eighteen, who had never been out of Kent, let alone England. It was decided that he and his father would go on ahead to Canada and prepare for the rest of the family, while the oldest son would stay behind to keep the butcher shop open as long as possible. Within two weeks, George and his father were working as farm labourers near Brandon, Manitoba.

Things went more or less as planned, although the elder

Shepherd decided to try the butcher business again, and the family ended up living in a small town in the Davidson area of the new province of Saskatchewan. The small business wouldn't support them all, so the older boys worked on farms. As soon as they could, they filed claims on quarter sections in the area. They broke land and met the requirements for homesteading, and within a few short years they managed to create a viable family farming business. But they soon discovered just how vulnerable grain crops were to the Canadian elements, so George's father decided they should diversify. He had heard of the ranching country in the southwest area around Maple Creek, where the climate was a bit more temperate and there was still plenty of grassland to be leased. The Shepherds filed a claim on another homestead there and set out to create a basic herd of beef cattle. Because they had some resources, they were able to cut down on the time the process usually took; it wasn't long before they were marketing steers.

George married and settled down on his own ranch there. Working with his father and one or two of his brothers, they built up the Shepherd ranch to be one of the major spreads in the south. There were ups and downs, of course, for a variety of reasons. Two world wars in the first half of the century, for example, had an impact on the family and their farming and ranching operations. George did not enlist for the First World War, but some of his brothers did. One returned with a permanent disability.

The family pulled together, though, and they survived the worst of times. Those times came in the Great Depression of the 1930s. First drought brought their businesses close to ruin, then the prices of everything they sold plummeted. George would recall in later years how the crushing weight of debt and poverty had a terrible emotional impact on prairie people, especially in the so-called dustbowl of southern Saskatchewan. But it also brought the community closer together. Like so many farmers from that era, he recalled the kindness of people, and the good times they would have, by getting together to sing and dance in defiance of the black cloud under which they were living.

War in Europe brought an end to the economic doldrums, just as the rains came back to the farm and ranch belt. Prosperity returned to the Shepherds and others. Grain prices rose and wartime jobs in the east recharged moribund industries. After the war George returned to one of his long-standing interests, local history. Fort Walsh, erected during the days of the whiskey traders as the headquarters of the North-West Mounted Police, was crumbling and in danger of disappearing completely. George became active in a movement to save the old stockade and refurbish the buildings to create a heritage site. His hard work and dedication were instrumental in unearthing the original design of the buildings, so the fort could be fully restored. It still stands today, a tribute to his determination.

Then personal tragedy struck. At around the age of sixty, still vigorous and healthy, he suffered a serious accident while operating a hay rake. His injuries were extensive and the nearest hospital was 105 kilometres away. It was a bad ordeal, and complications set in. He was transferred to Regina for more treatment and was in the hospital for about a year and a half. The injuries he suffered meant he would never be able to return to work on the ranch. With their family grown and out on their own, George and his wife left the ranch and moved to Saskatoon. There, they took in university students for room and board, until George was offered the post of curator at the Western Development Museum in 1953. He had made his interest in museums known, and the post was a dream job for him, marking the beginning of a second career that would occupy him for twenty-five busy years.

Funds were scarce and the museum, one of four branches of the provincially owned and operated institution, faced many challenges, but George plugged away, lobbying the government when he could, and tirelessly promoting the importance of preserving the past. At the time, the Saskatoon museum's collection was largely composed of the farm implements that had played such a large role in the opening of the west. George had had intimate contact with most of them, and his personal commentaries on the various displays became a highly valued part of a visit to the museum. He kept working at the museum's weak spots, eventually securing a better building, more storage, and a broader theme to the collection that included an authentic small town street. An active museum auxiliary group helped immeasurably, and before many years had passed, the Western Development Museum became one of the most important tourist attractions in Saskatoon.

George Shepherd left his mark in several areas of the province. Thankfully, his legacies live on to serve generations of the future.

Saskatchewan Archives Board S-B5517

Social Justice Crusader

SOPHIA DIXON

1900–1994

Sophia Dixon was a tireless worker in the cause of social justice.

*S*ophia Dixon believed passionately in social justice for all, equality for women, and world peace. She worked tirelessly for those causes throughout most of her ninety-four years, and lived to see many of the changes she sought actually implemented. Sophia continued, in her own quiet way, to speak out until the very end of her life. Though she earned public honours, she never sought acclaim. She contributed a great deal to Saskatchewan, pressing for growth of the co-operative movement, for publicly accessible and affordable health care, and for feminist causes—at the time taboo subjects—such as birth control information. Sophia was not deterred. She spoke out in a reasoned voice; she communicated her thoughts in her extensive writings; and she led by example.

Sophia Dixon began her life in Canada at age eleven, one of five children of a Danish immigrant couple who left their native land to escape poverty. As penniless homesteaders in the Kerrobert district, they found things to be little better in Canada. Young Sophia was forced to seek work as a servant in the homes of the few moneyed families in the area. Her earliest memories were of working twelve- to sixteen-hour days for $3 a week and having to put up with abusive, unsympathetic employers. The experience no doubt sowed the seeds of her lifelong concern with social justice issues.

Sophia survived the hard times of her youth, and even managed to learn English and take up the schooling she had been forced to abandon in Denmark. Indeed, she became such a good student that she was awarded a Governor General's Medal for the marks she achieved in grade ten. With grade eleven and three months of teacher training in Normal School, she began teaching in isolated country schools, living with a family in each of the districts in which she taught, and often walking miles to start a fire in a drafty, ice-cold country school. She had to deal with eight grades and all curriculum subjects, as well as satisfy the fussy school inspectors, who would drop in unannounced whenever they felt like it. She wrote years later that she was sure none of them had ever done such work, or had the faintest idea what it was like. They just insisted teachers be original and vital, prepare lessons from scratch and act like missionaries, never thinking of the meagre paycheques, and especially never thinking of unions.

Sophia's life changed considerably when she met and married Charles Dixon, a farmer from near Tramping Lake. Like herself, Charles was a reader with wide-ranging interests, including politics and social justice. Dixon had a car, and soon Charles and Sophia were attending meetings and taking a hand in the search for solutions to many problems facing Saskatchewan farmers. Radios, telephones, and automobiles were breaking down the isolation of rural dwellers. Sophia also learned about the struggles of other western women, such as Nellie McClung and Violet McNaughton, and she reached out to help whenever and wherever she could. As well, the "war to end all wars" had just been fought in Europe, and Sophia was intensely interested in assuring that conflict on such a scale should never happen again, for the sake of her own children—she and Charles had four children in four years—and for the sake of humanity as a whole.

The Dixons moved to a farm near Unity in 1926, and Sophia became involved with farm support organizations. She and Charles supported the Progressive Party of Saskatchewan (Progressives) and the Saskatchewan Wheat Pool, a farmers' operative formed to market pooled wheat collectively in order to protect farmers against the exploitation of grain companies and banks. Sophia attended a rally of the Progressives in 1927 where she met United Farmers of Alberta MP William Irvine and Agnes MacPhail, an MP for the United Farmers of Ontario—and Canada's first female Member of Parliament. MacPhail recognized Sophia's leadership qualities and became a friend and staunch supporter. When the Progressive Party disappeared, the Dixons turned to local independent groups working to better farmers' lives, such as the Farmers' Political Association of the South Battleford Constituency. The Dixons also became members of the Saskatchewan Branch of the United Farmers of Canada (UFC), and they became active in the CCF, a political party focused on ending poverty on the prairies, which was beginning to attract attention.

It was a time of action on many fronts. Five Alberta women— Emily Murphy, Nellie McClung, Louise McKinney, Irene Parlby, and Henrietta Evans—were launching what would be a successful bid to overturn a lower-court ruling that women were not persons under the law and therefore could not be appointed to the Canadian Senate. They had to go all the way to the Privy Council in England and the highest court of appeal for Canada, but they succeeded. On the fiftieth anniversary of that landmark event, Sophia Dixon received a Governor General's Award in recognition of her outstanding work in support of the co-operative movement and of rural women's organizations.

Sophia was active in the United Farmers of Canada for many years, first as director, then as women's president. She was also working with the CCF. She attended the founding convention in Regina in 1933, and actually had a hand in shaping the Regina Manifesto, a statement of the principles upon which the CCF was founded. She worked long and hard on the 1934 CCF campaign. Like many others, Sophia was disappointed when only a handful of CCF candidates made it to the provincial legislature. With the Depression taking its toll, she was forced to pull back from her work in the various organizations because she and Charles could no longer afford to pay for domestic help. The farm was still doing poorly after the Depression ended so Sophia and the children had moved to Saskatoon, which was the only way the Dixon children could get the university education their parents wanted for them.

Sophia rented a house and took in student boarders to make ends meet. Charles would come in for the winters, and Sophia found the time to take classes. After some problems had arisen in her children's school, Sophia decided to teach them at home. She felt that decision was validated when three of them graduated with degrees from the University of Saskatchewan in 1947. Coincidentally, Sophia completed her first year of university that same year. During this time, Sophia also joined peace groups and became active in the life of the community in several ways. She honed her writing style and became a regular contributor to the *Western Producer* and the *Saskatoon StarPhoenix*, as well as to some provincial and national periodicals.

Sophia's philosophical leanings, her communication skills, and her concern with social justice issues kept her involved in public life for many years. She worked on election campaigns and was Saskatoon's first returning officer in 1952. Sophia also became the first president of the Saskatoon Local Lodge of the Saskatchewan Farmers Union, on behalf of which she wrote a brief to the 1953 Royal Commission on Agriculture and Rural Life. She was a candidate—though never elected—for both the public school board and city council in Saskatoon. Health care was a long-standing concern for her, and she often spoke out on the need for birth control information for women. It was illegal for doctors to advise their female patients about birth control at the time and Sophia worked to have that law thrown out. It was taken off the books in 1969. She reflected on her battle in a 1986 address to the Saskatchewan Action Committee on the Status of Women:

> When doctors refused birth control advice, I couldn't be sure if they were really scared of two years in jail, or if they told the truth when they said they didn't know any- thing about birth control themselves. After all, if charged with an offence, they did have the option of saying they did it for a woman's health, and that the public good was served. Finally, an ex-army officer in family practice said I should try sitting up immediately after intercourse and cough real hard.... Maybe if sex had not been considered so sinful for generations, then today's problems with pornography might not have gotten so bad, and greed for

power might not have gone quite so far, leading even to wars.

Nettie Wiebe, an admirer and fellow activist, paid this tribute to Dixon in an article in *Briarpatch* magazine in 1994:

[Sophia Dixon's] life served as a fine illustration of her observation in the March 17, 1932 edition of the *Western Producer.* "Could anything be more natural and reasonable than that women, whose special business it has always been to minister to humanity as mothers, nurses or teachers, should share the work of reconstructing society on a safer and saner basis?"

Sophia Dixon left a large legacy in Saskatchewan.

Pioneer in Medicine

DAVID BALTZAN
1897 – 1983

Dr. David Baltzan, founder of the Baltzan Clinic in Saskatoon, was the first
physician in Saskatchewan to set up a practice in internal medicine.

P hysician, confidant, scholar, and teacher, Dr. David Baltzan was a diagnostician who lived for the challenge of pushing the envelope, for looking beyond conventional treatments and techniques. When he retired from medicine in the mid-1970s, the distinguished internal medicine specialist marked the end of a fifty-year career of service in Saskatchewan. Baltzan is remembered as a groundbreaker in his field—the first doctor in the province to specialize in internal medicine—and for his contribution to the health care of the nation as a member of the Hall Royal Commission, the group that laid out the blueprint for Canada's medical care system. Years before "Medicare" had even crept into the lexicon, Baltzan was searching for ways to make health care accessible to those unable to pay. Long before others had raised the alarm, it was David Baltzan who wondered out loud if there were links between smoking and heart disease. And it was Baltzan who placed the weight of his integrity behind early organ transplant programs while many others drew back from the ethical abyss.

The son of an immigrant family that fled anti-Semitism in Tzarist Russia, David spent his teenage years in a Jewish farming colony at Lipton, Saskatchewan. Wealthy landowners and traders in the old country, his father and uncles were ill-equipped for the hard life of a homesteader. They soon gave up on farming and moved to Saskatoon. The family started a fur and hide business which prospered, but David was interested in medicine. Eventually he extended his studies to the best schools in North America and Europe, in order to specialize in internal medicine.

When he returned to Saskatoon in the late 1920s, Dr. David Baltzan set up a specialty practice. He started out examining and treating anyone who would come to him, but as his reputation grew, referrals became the mainstay of the Baltzan Clinic. The medical community often questioned his judgment. Surgeons were kings in the "cut and cure" medicine of the day. But Baltzan was adamant in his belief that the future lay in scientific testing and in learning more and more about the many diseases that plagued humanity. For example, he stubbornly pursued a case of the so-called "blue baby syndrome," cyanosis, eventually establishing that the cause was a genetic abnormality, and not a physical defect, as had been previously believed.

Baltzan was a doctor with roots in small town medicine, who wrote off countless thousands of dollars in fees during the Depression. He was an academic with membership in scores of scientific societies, associations, and groups—his honours, accomplishments, and deeds are legendary. Although Jewish, Baltzan headed the most important committee in a Roman Catholic hospital for years. It was said that the sisters "treated him like a bishop." Although Baltzan epitomized innovative diagnostic techniques and sophisticated medicine, he saw himself in a somewhat different light. In his memoirs—which he never did finish—Baltzan characterized himself as just another prairie doctor, a pioneer in the tradition of family retainers who went where and when they were called, and did what they could within the limits of the science of their time. In reality though, Baltzan never accepted limitations. He achieved success and status that probably far exceeded his own expectations. Yet, as his close friend Emmett Hall said in his eulogy, Baltzan "never looked for credit and did most of those things—and more—as a volunteer."

Among the many goals he achieved was that of creating a family practice with his three sons, internists Marc and Richard, and surgeon Donald. They followed in their father's footsteps as respected physicians and teachers. The Baltzan name gained national acclaim after one of their patients received the first kidney transplant in Canada in 1963.

David Baltzan was known for high ethical standards in his medical practice, and he extended the same standards into his business life. As his practice grew, he put some of his assets into a broadly based investment portfolio. He was a careful investor and his net worth increased, but only under certain conditions. He believed his business interests should never compromise the integrity of his medical practice, and to that end he never did business in Saskatoon, where the clinic was located. He was notably upset when a cousin started a furniture store in the city using the Baltzan name, and upset again when his sons went into the hotel business in Saskatoon for a time, buying the venerable railroad hotel, the Bessborough.

However, David did enjoy the fruits of his labours. His family home was among the more opulent in the city, and he became something of a celebrity when, in his latter years, he acquired a Rolls Royce automobile. The stories about his somewhat erratic driving were probably overstated, but one in particular gained a kind of urban legend status around Saskatoon's University (now Royal University) Hospital. It was said that the administration finally allotted two parking spaces for Baltzan and his Rolls because no one wanted to park beside him and risk the dents and scratches he inflicted on nearby doors and fenders with alarming frequency.

David Baltzan died at age eighty-six in 1983. The Alzheimer's disease that took his life was perhaps the greatest frustration of his long and distinguished career. He battled the symptoms for several years, realizing, tragically, that the prodigious memory he had relied on was leaving him, and the intellect that had put him at the top of his profession was slowly eroding. He was eventually forced to leave his practice and, when he could no longer be cared for at home, entered a nursing home where he spent the last few years of his life.

But the Baltzan legacy lived on. The clinic he started continues to serve the people of the province and beyond. The library he collected was donated to the university. The many medical students whose lives he touched over the years perpetuated his wisdom and innovative approach. And happily, Dr. David Baltzan lived long enough to see the Medicare system that he helped create become a reality.

Mr. Hockey

MAX BENTLEY

1920–1984

Max Bentley pictured in front of a Hall of Fame photo showing him in his Maple Leaf uniform during his NHL days.

*I*n a post-war world hungry for good news stories and happy headlines, Max Bentley was a celebrity—regardless of how much he resisted fame. Stories abounded about how good Max Bentley was, at baseball, as a curler, and even as an owner of race horses. But it was hockey that seemed to be his favourite sport, and the one in which he left his mark. Short and light-weight, Max excelled at all parts of the game—except body checking—but he was especially adept as a skater. He had to be fast and elusive to survive on the ice when every opposing team had one or two big muscle-bound defencemen who stalked him relentlessly.

Travelling to Saskatoon in my father's car in my early teens, I remember always watching for the sign announcing the town of Delisle. That sign told the world (in big black letters) that Delisle was the home of the famous hockey-playing Bentley brothers. That would prompt my father to tell (or retell) his stories about watching Max Bentley and his brothers play hockey in Drumheller, Alberta. Like Father, I was a rabid hockey fan in those days of the six-team NHL (National Hockey League), when only the cream of the crop made it to the big time. Max was the *crème de la crème*—and one of our own, to boot.

Father had watched the Bentley brothers when they broke into semi-professional ranks in western Canada in the 1930s. He had a job in a coal mine in Drumheller one winter and the local hockey rink was the main gathering place for the town. The Bentleys were so good that Max's older brother Doug was invited to join the NHL's Chicago Black Hawks. The team passed over Max, the more skilled of the two, because he was small for the pros, weighing only about sixty-eight kilograms soaking wet. Also, a medical exam conducted by the team doctor for the Montreal Canadiens had mistakenly indicated that Max had some kind of a heart problem. That part of the story always made Father snort in indignation at the stupidity of that doctor. Then he'd relate with relish how Max earned the "Dipsy Doodle Dandy from Delisle" moniker that the sports scribes used every time they wrote about his many accomplishments.

Father felt an odd sort of kinship with Max Bentley, even though he'd never met the man. It had to do with the fact that the Bentley clan farmed just like Father did. One story especially resonated with Father. He'd read that Max was quoted as saying he was good with wrist shots because his wrists had become strong over the years from milking cows. He said he'd milked cows for two hours, morning and evening, all the time he lived at home. I think that, more than anything, endeared him to my father, who had also milked cows for most of his adult life. "How many of those other hotshots in the NHL have ever milked a cow?" he'd ask.

Max Bentley was one of those gifted individuals who seemed to play, effortlessly, a wide array of games requiring finely honed skills. He played semi-pro baseball in the summer. It was rumored that he could have had a career in either of the two top leagues in the States. Another neat story used to make the rounds about the Bentley brothers, when five of them played for one ball team. The story, recalled in a feature in the *Saskatoon StarPhoenix* when Max died, went like this:

> "I used to play baseball against the Bentleys," said Nick Metz, who was once Max's teammate with the NHL's Toronto Maple Leafs. "There were five Bentley brothers and you couldn't tell them apart. Max, who was the best, would get a hit, reach first base, and then there'd be a huddle of the five Bentleys. When the conference broke up, there would be a Bentley on first alright, but it always seemed to be Max who was batting again. Trouble was, we could never seem to prove it."

Max played twelve seasons in the NHL. In 646 games, he collected 245 goals and 299 assists for a total of 544 points. He won the Hart Trophy for most valuable player in 1945–46; the Lady Byng Trophy for the most gentlemanly player in 1942–43; and the Art Ross Trophy for scoring leader of the league in 1945–46 and 1946–47. His career is enshrined in the Hockey Hall of Fame, and true blue hockey fans still talk about his exploits.

Max Bentley broke into the big time after his brother Doug convinced the manager of the Chicago Black Hawks to give him a try. He quickly made the team and, along with Doug, became the scourge of opposing goalies from 1940 to 1947, with two years off for military service. In 1947, he was traded to the Toronto Maple Leafs. The trade so outraged Chicago fans that they stayed away in droves, sending the usually lucrative franchise into a slump for two or three seasons.

But it was a different story in Toronto, where Max led the team to three league championships over the next four years. He played in the NHL until 1954, putting in his last season with the New York Rangers before retiring to the family farm. But it wasn't really retirement, not quite yet. He was persuaded to take to the ice again for another three seasons, with the semi-pro Saskatoon Quakers.

Through it all, Max Bentley always preferred to stay out of the limelight. Compared to the star treatment players are accorded today, he managed to keep a relatively low profile. A quiet homebody, Max always came back to the farm and his wife and two sons during the off season. It was a time when players of his ilk gave their all, for love of the game more than for the money, so having a successful farm likely meant more in terms of future security than did the next contract in pro hockey. Besides (as Max frequently reminded the big-city media types who tried to put all the top players under the microscope) he was just a Saskatchewan farm boy at heart, who happened to love the game of hockey.

Max happily settled down to full-time farming after he finally hung up his skates for good in 1954. When he retired from farming, he and his wife Betty moved to Saskatoon, where they helped look after a subsidized housing development for seniors.

Max Bentley was the true hometown hero—a small-town boy making it in the big city. Kids were hushed in living rooms all over Saskatchewan on wintry Saturday nights, so the voice of Foster Hewitt could be heard bringing tidings of his latest hockey exploits, over crackling battery-powered radios.

They called it "putting the province on the map." It wasn't what he set out to do, but no one did it better than Max Bentley.

A Mystic, a Leader

MISTAHIMUSQUA (BIG BEAR)

1825–1887

Big Bear in 1886 while incarcerated at Stoney Mountain Penitentiary.

*A*lthough he never lived to see his territory become a province in Confederation, indigenous leader Mistahimusqua's wise counsel was relevant to negotiations that were ongoing through the twentieth century, and now continue into the twenty-first. A mystic, a respected leader of his people, and a visionary with a remarkably clear view of the fate that awaited the plains tribes, Mistahimusqua's warnings about the injustices of the treaty process (as well as the dangers of the rush to develop the west) still resonate. Several leaders from Saskatchewan's indigenous peoples community have left their mark since the first Europeans appeared in their midst about three hundred years ago, but few in as many important ways as Mistahimusqua, known to non-Natives as Big Bear.

Big Bear's childhood was typical of the Native culture of the times. It was an idyllic life, although for Big Bear the obligations of being the son of the chief brought him into the adult world at an earlier age than his peers. He was born Mistahimusqua in 1825, near what is now known as Jackfish Lake, some fifty kilometres north of the junction of the Battle and the North Saskatchewan rivers. Big Bear was the son of an Ojibwa man, Black Powder, and a woman who was either Cree or Ojibwa. His father, Black Powder, was chief of a small Cree band. The relationship between the Ojibwa and the Cree had for some time been getting closer. This was partly as a defensive strategy, in response to the power of the Blackfoot confederacy farther to the west, and partly because both the Ojibwa and Cree tribes had been evolving into Plains Indians to pursue the economic opportunities arising from the burgeoning fur trade. Mistahimusqua, or Big Bear, led the privileged life of a male child, enjoying the freedom of the nomadic lifestyle of his family. His first years were spent in pursuit of recreation, and absorbing the education that was passed down around the campfire in the evenings, as the elders told their tales.

The young man displayed an intense interest in the religious pursuits that were a strong influence on his father. It is not known whether he followed the tradition of going on a vision quest at an early age, but he did follow Cree and Ojibwa teachings that came to him through stories and legends. Big Bear also made a name for himself early on with his hunting prowess, and his courage and daring as a horse thief. Stealing horses from other tribes was a time-honoured activity—the first means by which young men established a reputation in the adult community. Big Bear embellished his image by giving away almost all the horses he brought home from his forays into enemy camps. He did this because of a dream he had, in which his people had been struck by disaster and left without homes or food. He interpreted the dream to mean he should not be preoccupied with possessions. As a young man, Big Bear became a charismatic figure, known as a visionary, good-natured and with a fine sense of humour. He married at an early age and directed his energies toward looking after his family.

Big Bear was small of stature. His face was permanently marked where he had survived smallpox at age twelve. The disease, introduced to the plains tribes by the Europeans with whom they traded, decimated many communities. Natives were especially vulnerable to smallpox, as they were to such diseases as measles, because they had no natural immunity. Big Bear learned something important early in his life from his brush with smallpox, as well as from witnessing first hand the consequences for many Natives of the illicit trade in whisky that had followed the fur traders. These experiences taught Big Bear that the arrival of European culture was something to be feared, as well as to be exploited.

As a youth Big Bear discovered something else that was bad news for the plains Indians: the insatiable appetite of white buffalo hunters, trying to satisfy faraway markets for hide and bones. The so-called "buffalo wars" dominated the lives of Big

Bear's people while he was growing up and after he assumed his role as chief, after his father died some time around 1865. However, the great event that awaited all the tribes and that would test his mettle and those of all Native leaders was the arrival of the railroad and European settlement.

The arrival of the rail lines heralded an influx of European settlers in the south. Settlement had already reached the area around the forks of the Red and Assiniboine Rivers. Roman Catholic and Methodist missionaries were fanning out across the plains, looking for converts and competing for government largesse. With Canadian government rule established in the west in 1869–70, the Cree and other bands began to consider negotiating treaties. The buffalo slaughter was continuing at an alarming rate and Big Bear and other Native leaders were getting a glimpse of their future. They were not pleased. Big Bear increasingly became the spokesman for Native needs and rights. At one point he had some two thousand individuals behind him in his tireless negotiations with government agents. He wanted to make sure the government would keep its promises to feed the bands and teach them to be farmers in exchange for huge tracts of land that had been traditionally owned by Natives—even though ownership was not a familiar concept to the bands.

Big Bear didn't get those assurances, however. He held out until his people actually began to starve. Finally, with great reluctance, Big Bear entered into a treaty agreement in December of 1882. Unfortunately, his worst fears were realized. Double dealing by government agents and callous disregard of the needs of his people left them worse off than before. Whenever Big Bear attempted to press his cause through diplomatic channels, the government responded by sending the police.

At the same time, the Métis of the Red River settlement were rising up against the Ottawa government, pressing for redress of their own long list of grievances. Led by a passionate advocate, the devoutly Catholic Louis Riel, they hoped to make common cause with Indian bands who were starving on reserves across the west. They contacted Big Bear to invite him to a gathering in 1884, but when government agents got wind of the plan they misunderstood, assuming that Big Bear was threatening to join a Métis uprising.

By spring of 1885, the conflict between Métis and police had flared into open violence with a battle at Duck Lake. The Métis were the clear winners. When word spread across the northwest, young warriors on reserves became restless. The warrior lodge in Big Bear's camp, led by a young hothead named Wandering Spirit, refused to listen to Big Bear's wise counsel to refrain. They led a march on the white settlement at Frog Lake. There, the group plundered a store, stole government horses, and took several white people prisoner. Inflamed by a cache of whisky they found, the warriors then confronted the Indian agent to demand food. When the agent refused, they shot him, along with ten other white people, again ignoring repeated pleas from Big Bear to put down their weapons. Next, they decided to attack Fort Pitt. Wandering Spirit and about 250 braves, with Big Bear close behind, threatened to burn the fort, but Big Bear interceded again. This time he was able to prevent bloodshed. The police were allowed to leave and the forty-some whites in the fort were taken prisoner before the braves torched the buildings.

A special force was deployed from Calgary to control these malcontents. A hit-and-run encounter took place at Frenchman Butte, but the special force caught up to the Cree at Loon Lake where a fierce fight ensued. Several of the Cree fighters were killed, a few escaped, and the rest surrendered. Big Bear, who had not taken part in the fighting, was arrested at Fort Carlton. Eleven Natives were put on trial for murder after the uprising. Eight were hanged. One Arrow and Poundmaker received three-year jail terms. One Arrow, old and very ill, was released after eleven months and died soon after. Poundmaker served only six months, then died of a lung hemorrhage.

Big Bear was also sentenced to three years, even though several white witnesses gave eloquent accounts of how he had saved the white prisoners when his young warriors had gone out of control. Big Bear himself gave a two-hour speech in which he reminded the court of his effort to keep the peace and his support for the rule of law. But the all-white jury took only fifteen minutes to find him guilty. He was sent to Stony Mountain Penitentiary. When a general amnesty resulted in the release of over thirty Indian rebels, he asked to be considered as well, but the authorities stubbornly refused, until he became seriously ill. Not wanting to pay the political price if Big Bear died in jail, they grudgingly released him. But he was a broken man, deserted by his own family, and without a home. He was taken as a guest on the reserve of his long-time friend Poundmaker, but died shortly after, at age sixty-two.

The federal government paid a price for its failure to treat Big Bear fairly. He became a martyr in the eyes of generations of Natives, and his name became a rallying cry in the battle to make a succession of governments live up to those early treaty promises. As a man of peace, he also earned respect in the white community. Many white people protested when government prosecutors, and then the jury, ignored Big Bear's passionate statement at his trial, pointing out that he had done everything he could to live by the law and to change with the times. Clearly, the legacy of Mistahimusqua, Native chief, known to Europeans as Big Bear, has strengthened the will of Natives and non-Natives alike, who believe in just treatment of Canada's first peoples.

The Mountain Builder

SID BUCKWOLD

1916–1998

Sid Buckwold during his term as mayor of Saskatoon, 1962–63.

*W*ell before it became the mantra of urban centres all over North America, Sid Buckwold was aware that urban growth and development would leave the city centre behind, a shell with no life. That was just one of Buckwold's many glimpses into the future, proven astute by events over subsequent years. A successful business operator with many ideas, Buckwold was often the right person in the right place at the right time. As a result, he raised the bar for local government politicians in Saskatchewan, before going on to a distinguished career as a member of the Canadian Senate.

Born in Winnipeg in 1916, Sid Buckwold was the son of a businessman who moved to Saskatchewan soon after Sid's birth, in search of opportunities. The family lived in Admiral for a time during Sid's childhood, later settling in Saskatoon where the Buckwold name became well known in the dry-goods industry. Sid attended elementary and high school in Saskatoon, and then went on to obtain a commerce degree at the University of Saskatchewan. He once told a reporter that his first choice was law, but family ties were strong and he wanted to be part of his father's growing business, which by then had several branches outside Saskatoon and Saskatchewan. Next, young Sid enrolled at McGill University, graduating with a Bachelor of Commerce with Great Distinction just in time to join the Canadian Army for four years of service in the Second World War.

Back home after the war, Sid joined one of his brothers and their father to focus on expanding the Buckwold empire, open-ing new branches in Winnipeg and Edmonton. By the early 1950s, he decided to enter public life. Saskatoon was a growing city with the usual development problems, but Buckwold believed it also had a secure future. The city needed leaders with a vision of how that future should be shaped, and Sid Buckwold fitted in well as an advocate of change.

Buckwold's first concern as a civic leader was to make the city a better place for people. One way he intended to do this was to open up a large area of the city centre for development. This would mean moving the CN (Canadian National Railway) station that had long dominated the area, as well as moving the CN rail line to the edge of the southern boundary of the city. Buckwold, by then mayor of Saskatoon, spearheaded a financing plan and conducted negotiations with CN over a period of several months, hammering out a scheme whereby the rails would be moved, a new CN station located just south of the city, and the CN Towers would go up on the old downtown site.

The new look to Saskatoon's downtown area began to take shape in 1962. It was a sweeping change that altered highway access from the west, and gave birth to a freeway that ringed the city. It brought the first modern shopping mall to Saskatoon, along with the twin CN Towers, which provided several floors of office accommodation, serving a wide range of professions. All in all, it was an accomplishment to look back on with pride. Buckwold was the man behind the new look, using his contacts to pave the way for the development with the passage of a special piece of legislation by the Saskatchewan government. The CN Towers, later known as Midtown Plaza, has undergone major expansion in the intervening years, but it continues to dominate the downtown business district.

In his quest to make the city a better place for people, Buckwold next turned his attention to the cultural life of his city. Ever the ardent supporter of the arts, he believed that Saskatoon needed a major auditorium and convention centre. Recognizing that the federal government would be distributing substantial sums to cities to help with the country's centennial celebrations, Buckwold began planning. The Centennial Auditorium was the result of that initiative. A major centre for professional touring groups of all kinds, home of the Saskatoon Symphony, and a centre that accommodates convention goers from near and far, the Saskatoon Auditorium stands as a monument to the foresight of its city council, at that time led by Sid Buckwold. In recognition of his contribution, the mainstage theatre in the facility was given his name. Buckwold was also instrumental in the building of the Mendel Art Gallery, one of Saskatoon's best-known amenities, referred to by Buckwold as "one of the jewels of Saskatoon." The project combined a major donation from Fred Mendel, owner of Intercontinental Packers, with a financing plan worked out by the city. Mendel also donated valuable works of art from his own collection, and the city moved its collection from the small publicly owned gallery that the new facility replaced. The Mendel Gallery has since become a major provincial centre for art display and gatherings of cultural groups.

But practical infrastructure issues were also on Buckwold's mind. It was through his efforts that Saskatoon took a major step forward in preserving the quality of water in the South Saskatchewan River. Buckwold insisted that the city had to invest in treatment of its sewage if it was going to be a responsible user of such a major water resource. He succeeded in getting all three levels of government to finance the necessary equipment. His powers of negotiation aided him in another of his famous exploits as mayor of Saskatoon, when he succeeded in creating a mountain.

By the time Sid Buckwold intrigued the country with an idea to "build a mountain out of a molehill," he had already made his mark nationally as the first-ever Saskatchewan president of the Canadian Federation of Mayors and Municipalities. With some serious lobbying—which earned him the "Salesman of the Year" award from a Regina sales and marketing club—Sid succeeded in bringing the 1971 Canada Winter Games to Saskatoon. It was a major coup for a small city, and the way it came about earned Saskatoon coast-to-coast publicity. Sid Buckwold, working with a small group of local innovators, came up with the idea to transform a flat area south of Saskatoon into a ski hill to be used as a major venue for the games. The imaginative project was accomplished by having city crews haul tons and tons of fill dirt to the site from various developments in the city. The work went on for many months and its supporters had to push hard to silence a few outspoken critics, but in the end the unlikely idea became a reality. Though in subsequent years the "mountain," named Mount Blackstrap, wasn't developed quite in keeping with Buckwold's original vision, it nonetheless continues to provide a beginner slope that is widely used and appreciated to this day.

Buckwold entered civic politics in 1953, serving as alderman until 1957. He became mayor in 1958 and held the job until 1963. He took time out to run, unsuccessfully, for the federal Liberal Party in the 1963 election, then contested a by-election the following year, again unsuccessfully. He returned to the civic stage in 1967, winning the mayoralty election that year and staying in that post until 1971, when he was asked by Prime Minister Pierre Trudeau to accept a seat in the Senate. He was an active senator until his retirement at age seventy-five, when he returned to his home in Saskatoon. Buckwold died at the age of eighty-four of a heart attack.

Sid Buckwold's legacy is alive and well in the city of Saskatoon and in the province as a whole—a legacy that reflects a life of extraordinary service and accomplishments.

The Western Oracle

JOHN DIEFENBAKER

1885–1979

John Diefenbaker at the 1975 sod-turning ceremony for
the Diefenbaker Centre in Saskatoon.

*S*tories abound about the tempestuous political career of John George Diefenbaker. Arguably, he became Saskatchewan's most celebrated son as he stubbornly rose from humble beginnings to the pinnacle of political power in Canada, the prime minister's office. However, despite his accomplishments in pursuing and winning power, to this day opinions still vary on what John Diefenbaker's real legacy was.

"What do you say about a larger-than-life legend like Diefenbaker?" I asked myself very early on the morning of 17 August 1979 as I drove to work at the *Saskatoon StarPhoenix*. As an editorial writer for the paper, I was alerted around 6:00 AM that Diefenbaker had died. The newsroom was racing to put a special package together to go to press on a deadline of 8:00 or 8:30 AM, and it was my job to write a tribute to the "Chief" and remake the editorial page. Needless to say, the clichés flowed throughout the coverage, in our paper and most others. It wasn't a time to analyze a political career that had begun with a bang, but had ended in acrimony and disarray. That would be left to his biographers.

Diefenbaker's reign as Progressive Conservative prime minister from 1957 until 1963 started slowly, but swelled into a wave of optimism that swept from coast to coast to coast. Popularly described as an "appointment with destiny," the Diefenbaker era was ushered in with promises of change—change that would put Canada on the map internationally, as well as set new standards of equality and progress domestically. Westerners in particular were ecstatic. "It's our turn," became the western mantra for those first heady days.

The Tory party had turned to the spellbinding orator from the prairies in 1956, giving him the leadership on a first-ballot victory at the Ottawa Coliseum on 14 December. But at first the voters of the country were less than enthusiastic with the new Tory leader. In the federal election six months later, voters gave the Tories a minority government after Diefenbaker toured the country and became known as "Dief the Chief." Diefenbaker chafed under the strictures of minority rule and went back to the people in February 1958 to ask for a majority. After his blazing country-wide campaign filled with promises of "new frontiers," and the dawn of a new era, John Diefenbaker swept back into power with the largest majority ever accorded a Canadian political party.

From that point on, the analysis depends entirely on who is doing the analyzing. Just as Diefenbaker was either loved or hated throughout his political career, his legacy is either exalted or vilified. Some say he squandered the opportunity offered through the record mandate he received. They believe his true genius was in winning power, not in exercising it with wisdom and vision. Others point to some of the highlights of the Dienfenbaker record, such as passing the Canadian Bill of Rights; giving the vote to Aboriginal peoples; his principled stand against South African apartheid at the 1961 Commonwealth Conference; appointing the Hall Commission, which paved the way for a national health care program; and his stand against letting the United States bring Bomarc missiles to Canada.

The argument will go on, no doubt. But regardless, John Diefenbaker made a permanent mark on the country and on his home province. Indeed, before Ottawa and the crucible of the prime minister's office, Dief's life had already assured him a degree of celebrity for its Horatio Alger quality.

Born to a schoolteacher father and a traditional, stay-at-home mother in 1895 at Neustadt, Ontario, young John became a westerner at an early age when his father was diagnosed with tuberculosis and advised to move to a dry prairie climate. The family lived in several small communities, finally settling in Saskatoon in 1910 so John and his brother Elmer would have access to schools, and to the university promised to the burgeoning town.

John's first claim to fame was his now legendary encounter

with the Canadian prime minister, Sir Wilfrid Laurier, in 1910. Diefenbaker was a paperboy for the Saskatoon daily and he approached Laurier to sell him a paper after the prime minister stepped off the train. He was paying a visit to do some politicking, as well as to lay the first stone in the building of the University of Saskatchewan. The story goes that John had committed himself to a life in politics at the tender age of thirteen, and that his chat with Laurier confirmed that promise in his own mind. Apparently it didn't influence his political loyalties, however. The following year he declared his support for the Opposition Conservatives, and never wavered.

Before the young John Diefenbaker made good on that first political promise to himself, he carved out a career in Saskatchewan as a defence lawyer. He interrupted his studies at the University of Saskatchewan to volunteer for the Canadian Army in 1916. He sailed to England with the rank of lieutenant, but was found to be unfit for service because of an irregular heart beat. A subsequent attempt to join the Royal Flying Corps failed for the same reason, so he returned to his studies and graduated in 1920. He set up a law office in Wakaw, then moved for a brief period to Vancouver, where he managed to get elected to the city council. Tragedy struck when Diefenbaker's fiancée died of tuberculosis in 1924. He was on the move again four years later, heading back to Saskatchewan and settling in Prince Albert where he opened another law practice. He began to attract attention in the Conservative Party the next year, winning the nomination in his home riding of Prince Albert for the October 1928 federal election. It was an unsuccessful bid, but he did create a stir by opposing some of the policies of the national leader of his own political party. Diefenbaker was suspicious of what he saw as a cosy relationship between the party establishment and Toronto's Bay Street. He was opposed to capital punishment and the leader was for it. He was interested in issues related to farming in the west, and the party was focused on Ontario.

During the ensuing years when Diefenbaker was trying—

unsuccessfully—to win seats both federally and provincially, his law practice thrived. He became a sort of "defence council of last resort," both in Saskatchewan and adjoining provinces, winning several high-profile cases involving capital crimes. It is said that it was during this period that he solidified his opposition to the death penalty, a cause he unflaggingly pressed throughout his careers in law and politics.

John Diefenbaker married Edna May Brower in Toronto in 1929 and they made their home in Prince Albert. Edna died in 1951 after a lengthy illness, and John remarried in 1953 to Olive Freeman Palmer of Toronto. She died in 1976 after suffering a heart attack. Only a few close friends ever knew the extent to which Olive's death devastated the aging Diefenbaker. Her demise came after twenty-three years of happy marriage and no doubt the grieving Diefenbaker was also moved to remember the other sad times in his life, when he lost his fiancée in 1924, and then Edna, his first wife and partner for twenty-two years.

Whatever else can be said of the life and times of John Diefenbaker, his record as a political campaigner is truly remarkable. He filled meeting halls wherever he went. Supporters and detractors alike were drawn to his piercing blue eyes and theatrical delivery on the podium. He was much loved in his home constituency. He won thirteen elections and was returned to the House of Commons for thirty-nine uninterrupted years. His majorities in his home riding of Prince Albert were consistently overwhelming. Small wonder he was often described as a political force by himself, and his party was more often referred to as the "Diefenbaker Party" than the Progressive Conservatives.

A Man for His Times

TOMMY DOUGLAS

1904–1986

Tommy Douglas was Saskatchewan's most acclaimed premier.

*C*harmer, pragmatist, dreamer, and doer, Tommy Douglas brought Saskatchewan into the twentieth century. The government Douglas led for seventeen years not only changed the face of the province of Saskatchewan, it set the pace for the whole of Canada, with innovative social policy, and especially with Douglas's greatest accomplishment, publicly funded health care. Douglas's powerful oratory played a part in these accomplishments, and he also made arguments that resonated with a majority of Saskatchewan residents.

Douglas pointed out the practicality of a good education system, and the advantages to all of having a resource of educated people. He argued that it was simple justice for the government to own the resources and to extend services, such as electricity and natural gas, into farming areas by using profits from selling gas and electricity in the towns and cities. And he made a clear case for affordable and accessible health care simply by pointing to the inadequacies and injustices in private care. The sick understood because most couldn't pay for the care they needed. Parents understood because they lived in fear of having a sick child and not having the money to pay for treatment. Even doctors understood, because most had thousands of dollars in uncollected accounts and daily had to choose between treating patients for free or turning away those in need.

One of the more interesting aspects of the Douglas story is the extent to which the wily premier—so widely vilified as a radical socialist—actually wrought an economic miracle in the poorest of poor provinces by wooing entrepreneurs to come in and invest in mines, in oil, and in businesses.

I had the good fortune in the early 1970s to be granted an interview with Tommy Douglas. I was working at the *Yorkton Enterprise* newspaper. The community was hosting a special day of tribute to Douglas, icon of prairie politics, so I asked the organizers if they would arrange a time for me to talk to him. I didn't really expect the interview to happen, but true to his reputation as one of the most accessible politicians in the country, Douglas agreed to talk to me. We would meet in the motel room that had been reserved for him for the day, as a place where he could go for a rest when crowds and heat became overwhelming.

Douglas spent the long sun-baked afternoon working the crowds on the old Yorkton Agriculture Exhibition Grounds. I lurched around in his wake, astounded at his energy, until about midafternoon, when I had to find some shade and a cold drink. Douglas, however, soldiered on, shaking hands as if he were on the last day of a close election campaign. He seemed to know most of the people he met, and the adulation was palpable. There was a picnic supper followed by speeches, including a barnburner address by Douglas. He vilified the Trudeau Liberals, the Opposition Tories, the welfare bums of Bay Street, and the Liberal Party of Saskatchewan. The crowd was enthralled. Well into his sixties at the time, Douglas had flown from Ottawa to Regina, then travelled by car to Yorkton, before spending the day with his admirers. Someone with less stamina would have been exhausted.

I knocked on the door of his motel room at the appointed time, half expecting an aide to appear to tell me that Tommy Douglas was too tired to talk. Instead, he met me at the door with a wide grin, insisted I take the only chair in the room while he sat on the bed, and asked me what I wanted to talk about. There was plenty to talk about. As national NDP leader, Douglas had recently made the news by attacking American policy in Vietnam and protesting the use of the War Measures Act in Canada. The NDP was still widely regarded as the conscience of the nation, and Douglas was in the process of turning over the leadership to David Lewis. But after that tribute day of nostalgia in Yorkton for the Douglas era in Saskatchewan, the only thing I could do was ask him to reminisce. Had he been afraid in 1944 when he left the security of his Member of Parliament seat in Ottawa to become the premier of one of the poorest provinces in Canada?

"No," he laughed. "I didn't know enough to be afraid. Anything seemed possible back then." The feisty Baptist preacher, with a boxing championship in his background, had watched depression and drought ravage southern Saskatchewan in the Dirty Thirties. The church had hemmed him in and hampered his work for social change, so he switched to the state, heading off to Ottawa in 1935 as a CCF Member of Parliament.

Although he made his mark rhetorically in the stodgy House of Commons, Douglas was still impatient with the pace of change. By 1944, the Saskatchewan CCF party badly needed new blood. The war was ending, times were changing fast, and Douglas finally saw opportunities to work toward the society he dreamed of, where his creed "to each according to his need, from each according to his ability to pay," might finally mean something. The 1944 Saskatchewan election was almost a coronation for the popular CCF leader and his earnest band of farmers, teachers, labourers, and others who wanted to cut old ties with banks and big business and "do politics" for ordinary people. They were heady days, but the problems were enormous. Saskatchewan was $178 million in debt (the equivalent of $17 billion today). Saskatchewan couldn't borrow a dollar anywhere.

Tommy Douglas made no bones about using his powers of persuasion to get the corporate world on board. The trick, he said, was for government to always maintain its regulatory role, and to never give up ownership of resources that rightfully belonged to the public. That night in Yorkton, Douglas looked back on those days, as the hour planned to talk to me stretched into two hours. An anxious Lorne Nystrom, then the rookie NDP MP for Yorkton, kept coming in and interrupting Tommy to remind him that they still had to drive back to Regina that night. Douglas ignored him, seeming to become energized as he relived the political battles of a quarter century earlier.

"You're a newspaperman, you'll like this," he said at one

point, fairly squirming with mirth. "The newspapers hated us CCFers and they opposed us at every turn. I'd make a speech; the *[Regina] Leader-Post* would send a reporter to cover it; then take the reporter's copy and insert editor's comments after every one of my statements to say why it was wrong, or misleading, or whatever—short of committing libel.

"They never seemed to catch on that they were actually helping us. The public disliked and distrusted the newspapers' wealthy owners more than they disliked and distrusted us, so the more the editors called us commies, pinkos, etc., the more the public got on our side."

Tommy Douglas's ability to observe, understand, and put to use such attitudes was just one of many factors that contributed to his success. His popularity and record of accomplishments have been unmatched since his era. Tommy Douglas was truly a man for his times.

Rebel with a Cause

GABRIEL DUMONT

1838 – 1906

Gabriel Dumont pictured sometime in the 1880s, the tempestuous decade
during which he helped lead his people in the infamous Riel Rebellion.

*F*iery Gabriel Dumont was at the centre of the Métis uprising in Saskatchewan, and had been its military leader for
many years. His problem was that he was illiterate and lacked
the oratorical skills needed to press his case in Ottawa. When we
hear or read about the North-West Rebellion of 1885, the story
is dominated by Métis martyr Louis Riel and his fate at the hands
of an all-white jury. But to many Métis people, and to some
historians, the name Gabriel Dumont deserves equal billing.

Dumont was born in 1838 beside the Red River south of
Lake Winnipeg. By the time he was two years old, his parents
were feeling surrounded, as settlers began to take over the Red
River Valley. They moved west to Saskatchewan country, settling
near Fort Pitt. There, they found the freedom they loved, and
young Gabriel grew up in traditional fashion. By age ten he had
learned to shoot a bow and arrow with enough accuracy to
attract the attention of his adult relatives. He also became an
expert canoeist, fisherman, hunter, and trapper. It was an idyllic
existence. Life was good, with plenty of buffalo, the staple of
Métis life—just as they were for their Indian neighbours. A sturdy
youth with dark curly hair, Gabriel made a reputation for himself as a fearless horseman while still in his teens. He learned to
hunt with the best of them, recklessly charging into the stream of
stampeding buffalo to claim his share of the spoils. Gabriel
Dumont's biographers have credited him with many legendary
exploits in those teenage years, including the claim that he killed
a man when he was just thirteen. The story goes that Indians
were attacking the Métis camp and Gabriel fired on a brave who
was about to kill his (Gabriel's) father. Gabriel also spent time
with his mother's people, the Sarcee, and learned Cree and
French, along with three or four other dialects used by the plains
tribes. Métis culture of the time attached no importance to

literacy. Métis men were judged on their physical prowess and courage rather than their eloquence with the written word, so young Gabriel was not taught to read or write, something that would haunt him in later life.

At the age of twenty-one, Gabriel Dumont married eighteen-year-old Madeleine Wilkie, a woman of Scottish and Indian ancestry. They never had children of their own, but adopted a little girl believed to be related to Madeleine. By the time he reached his mid-twenties, Gabriel, the undisputed leader of the hunt, was chief of the Métis in the Saskatchewan area. A large man as an adult, Gabriel loved dancing to fiddle music and was known as an inveterate card player and gambler. Both Gabriel and Madeleine were deeply religious. He was also known for his generosity, always giving part of his buffalo kill to his less fortunate neighbours.

By 1868, however, the buffalo herds were thinning out and the inevitable march of settlement was changing the free life the Métis had enjoyed. Acting on the advice of a visiting priest, Dumont decided his group should establish a more permanent village and position themselves to lay claim to the land they had been living on. That process was Dumont's preoccupation for the next few years. At the same time a long-simmering dispute flared up in Manitoba, sounding alarm bells among the Saskatchewan Métis group. In 1870, the Métis at Red River, led by firebrand Louis Riel, rose up and established a provisional government. They made a brave attempt to claim their rights, and for a time it looked like the attempt would succeed, but ultimately the Canadian government broke the promises it had made as a way of ending hostilities. The Métis government was ousted and Riel was forced to flee to Montana, while many of the Red River Métis drifted west and settled in Dumont's area.

By 1872, Dumont had staked out some land near Batoche on the South Saskatchewan River. He was also promoting an alliance between the Métis and the Indian bands in the area. When they fell on hard times, he helped with food. Dumont started a ferry business and began to do some farming. Along with his hunting and fishing, he was able to make a respectable living. But when Gabriel Dumont headed up a drive to form a local government and set up a framework of simple laws that the community would live by, he was tempting fate; when he tried to impose those laws on some traders from outside the area, they complained to the federal government. So were sown the seeds of the North-West Rebellion.

Dumont was scheduled for arrest, but was exonerated in the end. The local government was disbanded in 1875, and the problems were escalating. Fort Battleford was constructed within two years, to serve as the capital of the North-West Territories; treaties were signed giving Indians reserve land, but nothing was granted to the Métis. When the government tried to impose a toll on all wood cut on Crown lands, Dumont led a protest that succeeded in having the toll struck down. He also led an initiative to petition the government to exempt the Métis from homestead regulations so their long, narrow farm sites, fronting on the river, would be recognized. The petition was ignored.

For years, a remote federal government had been ignoring legitimate Métis claims. Also ignored were claims of status Indians in the west. The Métis were pushed to the limit. But the battlefield was not the first choice for Dumont. Indeed, the record shows that he exhausted other means of getting redress for years of mistreatment at the hands of politicians and white society in general. When status Indians were granted reservation lands, though land ownership was still denied to the Métis, Dumont saw the writing on the wall. His followers, furious with what they saw as an oppressive system, were not prepared to wait for diplomacy to work.

By 1884, several hundred Métis, with Dumont still in a leadership role, were demanding title rights from the territorial council. They also dispatched a four-man delegation to go to Montana to get Riel to come back to Canada and be their leader. When he agreed, the groundwork was laid for rebellion.

It seems highly unlikely that the Métis, in the end, could have defeated government forces. However, had Dumont's strategy played a bigger role in the planning, the encounter may at least have taken a significantly different course. He favoured a more aggressive approach, taking the fight to the police, and then to the forces led by General Middleton. But he yielded to Riel, who argued that if the Métis forces waited until they were attacked, God would protect them. Dumont capitulated, partly because he had acquired a deep respect for the charismatic Riel and the great courage Riel had shown by standing up for the Red River Métis in 1870. The Métis families that left the Red River settlement to join Dumont's community sang Riel's praises, and he was well on his way to becoming a legend in his own time. But Dumont yielded to Riel's battle plan also because he needed Riel and feared alienating him. Unable to read, Dumont felt the sting of his own inadequacy at not being able to present his case to the government in writing. Riel was a skilled communicator and knew precisely what to say.

The course of the battle, Dumont's heroic role, and the eventual outcome of the rebellion are well known by Canadians. In the end, the government focused on Riel, and he was tried, convicted, and sentenced to hang. Dumont was exiled to Montana, where he made an unsuccessful attempt to organize a prison break to save Riel's life. Madeleine died during those years of exile, and Dumont dropped out of sight until he became part of a Wild West show. Ironically, as long as there was a price on his head in Canada he was popular with American audiences. He turned down a chance to accompany the show to England, fearing the British would arrest him and send him back to their "colony" for a trial. Even after the Canadian government issued a general amnesty for the participants in the rebellion, Dumont was still mistrustful. He waited for eight more years before finally returning to Saskatchewan in 1893. He lived quietly on a farm owned by a relative in the Batoche area.

What's remarkable about Gabriel Dumont's story is this: the cause of Métis rights for which Dumont and others fought continues to be an open wound in Canada. As recently as 2003, Canadians awaited a Supreme Court decision on the question of whether Métis people should have the same hunting rights as status Indians. Again, as governments edge toward the granting of self-governance to Native bands across the country, the Métis are left in limbo.

Gabriel Dumont died in May 1906, after going on a hunting trip. An obscure figure by then, his passing attracted little notice outside of Métis circles, though Métis from all over the northwest gathered for his funeral, overflowing the small church in Batoche that had served as rebel headquarters in the battles twenty-one years earlier.

Inspired Painter
ERNEST LINDNER
1887–1988

Ernest Lindner shown at work on his art, the activity that consumed him for most of the long life he enjoyed in Saskatchewan.

Let us not be just contributors to the world's stomach with our wheat, and to the world's industry and armaments with our minerals. Let us contribute to the world's cultural life with thoughts, with literature, music, folk songs, handicraft and art— grown on our own native soil. Only if we do that will we live a full life, will we truly appreciate the cultural accomplishments of other nations and other times and become a full member in the family of great nations of the world.

—Ernest Lindner in a radio broadcast,
No Civilization Without Creative Art

With those few words, Saskatchewan painter Ernest (Ernie) Lindner encapsulated his world view and his vision for an enlightened future. And they weren't just words in a script. Lindner dedicated his life and his remarkable body of work to the building of the kind of egalitarian society in which he believed. His was a life lived with purpose and passion, and his legacy has touched millions around the world.

In later years, Ernie Lindner recalled that his interest in art had started when he was only three or four years old. Born 1 May 1897 in Vienna, Austria, Ernie was the son of a business-man. He was expected to join the firm and carry on his father's work when he was finished school. He tried. Although the idea did appeal to him of designing the walking sticks produced by the firm, Ernie found the firm's business end to be stifling. He left the business and went into military service, rising to the rank of lieutenant in the Joint Austrian Air Force from 1915 to 1918. After the war, still restless and without direction, he first tried his hand at banking, then he became part owner of a chocolate factory, but Ernie was still searching. He concluded that he wouldn't find what he was after in the old, stodgy society of Europe. He decided to emigrate to Canada, and he ended his marriage at the same time.

Ernie came to Saskatchewan, where he found work as a labourer on a farm near Markinch. After a few years of hard work, he had a grasp of the English language and was ready to move on. Saskatoon was his next stop, and, as it turned out, his permanent home. Again Ernie turned to menial jobs to make a living. House painting was one of the first things he turned his hand to, although he proved to be rather inept at it. In his spare time, he pursued an old hobby, sketching and drawing. In 1928, Gus Kenderdine, resident artist at the University of Saskatchewan, saw some of Lindner's work and encouraged him to develop his talent. By 1931, he was able to find work in art education, thinking it would just be a stopgap until he could find a better job. Lindner didn't have any training—as an artist or a teacher—so he made it up as he went along.

Ernie Lindner would go on to a thirty-year teaching career, leading what amounted to a revolution in art and art teaching in the province of Saskatchewan. Within five years of getting that first part-time teaching post, one night class had grown to five plus a few day classes. Lindner's teaching methods were unconventional by any standards. He assessed each student on his or her particular interests and talents, attempting to give each student individual instruction. The results he achieved were most gratifying, to him as a teacher, to his students, and to the school system that employed him.

In 1934, Lindner built a cottage at Emma Lake, where he found inspiration for his painting in the seasonal changes of the forest. Later, the Emma Lake Art School sprang up there, and a nearby land formation was named Lindner Point in Ernie's honour. By this time, he was remarried, with an infant daughter. He painted obsessively whenever he found the time. He found ready markets in galleries across the country and beyond as he gained recognition for his depictions of the natural world, his spiritual home. At the same time, he further honed his teaching skills and reached out into the community as a whole. He started weekly gatherings at his home, called simply "Saturday Nights," to critique the art of those who attended, and to indulge in wide-ranging discussions about art, politics, and all manner of cultural issues—whatever his guests wished to put on the table. Saturday Night at Ernie's became a treasured ritual for the intelligentsia of the city, thriving for some thirty years.

As an educator, Ernie Lindner campaigned actively for the acceptance of art as a subject of matriculation at the University of Saskatchewan. In the 1940s, he drew up the art curriculum for Saskatchewan high schools. Lindner influenced a generation of artists, among them Native artists, who went on to successful careers in all branches of the arts. He was a passionate advocate of social democracy. After the CCF came to power in Saskatchewan, Lindner was instrumental in the creation of the Saskatchewan Arts Board. Throughout his life he promoted the notion that art belonged in the community, that it was part of a balanced and happy life.

Lindner worked full-time as an artist from 1962 to1988. Along with his painting, he became known for his engraving and for his watercolours. His works have been shown throughout Canada, and internationally at Canada House Gallery, in London, England, and at Canadian cultural centres in Paris and Brussels. Among the many awards he received throughout his lifetime are an Honourary Doctor of Law Degree from the University of Saskatchewan (1972); a membership in the Order of Canada (1979); and a Life Time Award for Excellence in the Arts from the Saskatchewan Arts Board he helped to establish (1988).

Ernest Lindner died in Saskatoon in 1988, but his legacy lives on. Artists still find inspiration at his Emma Lake haunts; the art he created can be seen in private collections and public displays; his views on nature conservation continue to influence public policy; and his contributions to the education system are entrenched.

Judy Levasseur/Village of Edam

Farmer, Bootlegger, Poet
WALTER FAREWELL
1879–1955

Walter Farewell's cramped lean-to home behind the village cafe (now located at Edam's future museum site) was a centre for gambling and late-night booze parties.

People have contributed in a wide variety of ways to Saskatchewan communities. Some were heroic and widely acclaimed, some were inclined to modest lives in which their good works were of a more subtle nature, while others made their mark by their individuality and through creative works. At the extreme end of this passing parade were the few whose contributions weren't even recognized until long after they were dead.

Among that small number was Walter Farewell, homesteader, bootlegger, town roustabout, and, to the great surprise of many, poet and chronicler of his own life and times and that of his hometown of Edam, Saskatchewan. Edam could be described as an unspectacular, rather typical prairie village that, ironically, may have been vaulted into its most visible moment by the member of the community who during his lifetime was the least regarded or cherished. However, it wasn't until folklorist and historian Michael Taft carried out extensive research on Farewell's life and legacy, and published the book *The Bard of Edam* in 1992, that Farewell's work was available to the public.

Farewell was an intensely private man who seemed to be especially uncommunicative about his greatest preoccupation, poetry writing. Not that he had close friends in whom he might have been inclined to confide. His best buddies were his drinking and poker companions, and they were not of a literary bent. Farewell was, though. It is not clear how or why Walter Farewell became so knowledgeable about the great writers of his time, and so obsessed with recording the story of his own life in verse. The mystery of Farewell's character was compounded by the fact that, as far as anybody knew, he had never attempted to get any of his work published, nor did he make any attempt to assure that it would be found after his death. It came about more or less by accident that three scribblers containing his poems were dis-covered amongst his effects after he died. An astute Edam citizen realized she had come upon a treasure.

Farewell's poetic legacy was of greater value for its gritty, firsthand accounts of the hard life of a homesteader, and the underbelly of life in a small town, than it was for literary merit. As a writer, his work might best be described as rough around the edges, in the style made famous by the great northern chron-icler, Robert W. Service. Farewell told stories; he struck out at those institutions and individuals he despised; and he ruthlessly assessed his own failures and shortcomings, all in verse. It made for interesting poetry revealing much about the man, his imme-diate environment, and his times.

By the time Taft started looking into Farewell's life some thirty-five years after his death in 1955, few Edam residents remembered much about the man. Some believed he had come to the area as a remittance man. Remittance men were British subjects whose wealthy families wanted to get rid of them for one reason or another and sent them to the new land of Canada to live on small stipends, safely out of the way. Farewell did have a bit of an English accent and obviously had education in the classics, two factors that supported the assumption that he was from a wealthy British family. But Taft traced the Farewell roots to Ontario. The record isn't complete, but he likely came from the Colborne area, near Oshawa, the descendant of an American family of United Empire Loyalists who had fled the United States after the Revolutionary War. The sketchy records indicate that his parents, and likely his grandparents, were engaged in farming. In his poetry, Walter made oblique references to some of his ancestors and family members. In particular, his writings give evidence of a strong distaste for American culture, history, and politics. He championed king and country, as he watched from afar Britain's role in the Boer War, the First World War, and the Second World War.

Like many young men of his day, Farewell was unable to find a job or a business opportunity in the province of his birth, so in

1902, at just twenty years of age, he ventured west to the new province of Manitoba. He first stopped in a place called Griswold, a small community with a large population of Ontario expatriates, where he probably worked on threshing crews at harvest time. More to his liking, however, was his work as a printer's devil, an errand boy and jack-of-all-trades combined, for the town's weekly newspaper. That job may have been Walter's entree into a career of journalism, but fire destroyed much of the town, including the newspaper office, so he was on the move again.

Farewell then returned to his farming roots and moved farther west where free land was still to be had, in the even newer province of Saskatchewan. He settled on a homestead a few kilometres from the town of Edam in 1906, and there he stayed, battling the weather, the banks, the machinery companies, and his own addictions to liquor and gambling. His often poignant poems tell of the extreme poverty he endured in the cramped dugout home he shared with throngs of mice and hordes of bedbugs, fleas, and lice. He could barely keep from freezing in the winter, and mosquitoes and grasshoppers plagued his summers. For weeks, his diet would consist of nothing but pancakes he concocted out of flour and water. His oxen died, his only horse succumbed, and his machinery was repossessed. The Great Depression nearly did him in, but even when farming became more prosperous during the war years, and his neighbours were paying off their debts and expanding, Farewell found ways to squander the money that did come his way.

Unmarried and without prospects—the one woman he fancied from afar likely never even knew he was alive—Walter had only his poetry for solace, and he poured his heart out in verse. The greedy bankers, the two-faced machinery salesmen, and the uppity snobs of Edam who had little time for the ragged recluse who got drunk and spouted poetry—he railed at them all. For example, he was especially vitriolic in a poem entitled simply "Edam":

Oh holy Edam! Wondrous Gem!
Thou little new Jerusalem!
All sorts of grafting crooks abound,
There's much that's rotten, little sound
The men are worse than bulls or boars,
The women—most of them are whores;
And truth, no more by cunning mastered,
Would prove near every child a bastard.

But when things became blackest, Walter found a new and uniquely appropriate source of revenue, one that didn't depend on the weather or the bankers. He became a bootlegger. Farewell made and sold home brew for years, only rarely getting into trouble with the Mounties—even though prohibition was in effect for much of his bootlegging career.

Eventually Farewell gave up all pretences of farming, sold what was left of his land, and moved into town. He worked for years in the cafe, serving meals and cleaning in return for cramped living quarters in a lean-to attached to the building. He and a friend kept the bootleg business going and Farewell's little lean-to home became the centre for gambling and late-night booze parties, none of which endeared him to the town's upper crust. But Farewell had little time for reformers and teetotallers, seeming quite content with the company of his poker friends and the consumers of his high-octane home brew. This life of revelry lasted for fourteen years, until he had a row with the cafe owner and was not only fired, but also evicted. His next venture was to rent the town pool hall, which he operated, both as a place to play pool and poker, and a convenient domicile for his illicit booze business. It seemed like a good arrangement.

Throughout, Farewell recorded his thoughts in verse. His production slowed as he got older and was sober less of the time, but he did leave his thoughts on the page occasionally, as in this short, self-mocking poem, "Rugged Old Duds":

These rugged old duds may not be the most pleasing,
But in spite of that fact they will keep me from freezing:

The weather's too tough to wear fig leaves like Adam,
And so though they're awful, I'm glad that I had 'em.

The things he was writing would certainly have startled the
townspeople. If they acknowledged him at all, the people of
Edam regarded Walter Farewell as little more than an unwanted
fixture.

Walter Farewell died in the local hospital at seventy-six years.
He was ill for only a few days. His passing was as unremarkable
and unmarked as his life had been. It wasn't until the contents of
his scribblers full of poetry became public property that
Farewell's role in the life of the community came into focus. Taft's
title for Farewell, *The Bard of Edam*, fits this enigmatic individual.
More of Walter Farewell's life remains a mystery than the part we
know. Nonetheless, Farewell left his mark, in a way no one would
have ever foreseen.

Anti–TB Crusader

ROBERT GEORGE FERGUSON

1884 – 1964

Robert Ferguson led the battle in Saskatchewan
against the feared killer, tuberculosis.

orking for the Saskatchewan Anti-Tuberculosis League put a young preacher-turned-doctor, George Ferguson, in the front lines of a battle that no one knew exactly how to mount. One of the cornerstones of Ferguson's commitment to that battle was that nobody in need would be turned away.

When Saskatchewan officially became a province of Canada in the early 1900s, it had a large territory, a small but optimistic population, and one major public health problem: TB (tuberculosis). Tuberculosis was an inexorable killer in the days before antibiotics. Its victims often suffered for years and infected many others before even being diagnosed. The only known treatment was total rest for lengthy periods and the only institutions offering specialized care were in the United States. Saskatchewan's three small hospitals did not have the resources to deal with TB patients. Very few of those who needed treatment could have afforded to be hospitalized anyway. Statistics from those first years show that the province was losing upwards of four hundred people a year to TB, with another one thousand incapacitated by the disease, out of a population of around seven hundred thousand.

The Saskatchewan Anti-Tuberculosis League was formed in 1911 by a group of doctors, politicians, and concerned citizens. The goal was to build a sanatorium. The fledgling provincial government offered some help, but the program relied mainly on public donations. Although the idea of taking action against the scourge of TB enjoyed wide public support, actually raising the money was a different matter. The vast majority of the people of the province were not wealthy. Many were impoverished. The fund-raisers could get pledges, but little cash. As well, over half of the would-be donors had to forfeit on their pledges. Two years later the deeply indebted league eventually got a construction program going at the site they had selected at Fort Qu'Appelle, near Regina. It wasn't until 1917, when soldiers began to arrive back from overseas needing treatment for TB, that the institution actually began to treat the sick. Fort Qu'Appelle Sanitorium would become locally known as "Fort San" or simply "the San."

While the war was the catalyst, the soul of the anti-TB battle was Robert George Ferguson, the man hired to be interim superintendent of Fort Qu'Appelle Sanatorium. A young medical doctor who had gained experience while working in Winnipeg with the Manitoba TB treatment program, Ferguson came highly recommended. The sanatorium board originally contracted Ferguson for six months, after which time they expected the incumbent to return from overseas service to resume his duties. Instead, the incumbent resigned, preferring to live in England. Ferguson had made such an impression on the board that he was immediately appointed as full-time superintendent, a job he held until his retirement in 1948.

Dr. Ferguson (he used the first name George) threw himself into the task of getting the new institution up and running. Known for his administrative skills, he was also an accomplished researcher and clinician. The battle against TB had personal meaning for the young doctor. The sixth child of a family of sixteen, he had lost two siblings to the disease when he was growing up on the family farm in North Dakota, about twenty-four kilometres south of the Canada–United States border. George himself had survived diphtheria in his early years. The disease left him with chronic bronchitis and a hoarse throat, a condition that forced him to give up the religious ministry that had been his first career choice after leaving the family farm. In later years, George would say that he redirected his evangelistic zeal into the fight against TB.

The Ferguson family came to Canada shortly after the turn of the century, settling in the Yorkton area. Ever the bookworm, and a promising student when his farm work had allowed him to attend classes, George moved to Winnipeg. His goal there was to obtain senior matriculation and soon a career in the Methodist ministry. When preaching proved to be too much of a strain on his husky voice, he enrolled in the Manitoba College of Medicine in 1912 and graduated near the top of his class in 1916. George and Helen, his fiancée of four years, were married that same year. George began his medical career by working as assistant superintendent of the municipal hospitals in Winnipeg. When the Fort San search committee was looking for an interim superintendent, George came highly recommended by his immediate supervisor. So began what turned out to be the life work of Dr. George Ferguson.

Finances were always precarious in those first years, with the only certain source of funds coming from the federal government for treatment of soldiers. The federal government also paid for the treatment of the Natives who were admitted to the San, but their numbers were very small at first. Otherwise, the $2.50 daily charge to patients was almost all the responsibility of the individual. The provincial government made a small contribution, but the patient had to pay the balance. The only help came from their home municipalities. Municipal governments of Saskatchewan had agreed to a system where they paid a stipend for indigents from their areas. But since TB was a disease that was especially prevalent among the poorest, that still left many whose bills never did get paid. One of the cornerstones of Ferguson's commitment to the battle was that nobody in need would be turned away.

As head man, it fell to him to juggle the finances, maintain a small but dedicated staff, and provide the standard of care that would effectively combat TB. At the same time, he knew that if the assault on the disease was to be successful, there would have to be a massive preventive element. Public education, an increased awareness of the dangers of TB, and a program of early diagnosis were the essential elements. As well, new medical techniques were being developed that required upgrading of skills for Ferguson and his medical assistant.

As superintendent, George Ferguson lived in a house on the grounds of the San. He was on call twenty-four hours a day. His was truly a hands-on administration. Patients and staff from that time recall that Ferguson pitched in wherever there was a need. Among other things, he was often seen opening mail, peeling vegetables, looking after the heating system, and finding time for the odd chess game with a patient. Ferguson was also known for his great compassion. He would often sit at the bedside of a dying patient around the clock.

Ferguson got stuck in the snow one stormy winter night and trudged through the drifts to a stranded passenger train. On board was a group of travelling salesmen, all members of the recently founded Association of Canadian Travellers. They happened to be looking for a public service project, and when Ferguson told them about the difficulties he was encountering trying to keep Fort San going, while finding money for preventive measures in the fight against TB, they immediately got involved. Eventually a Prince Albert radio station took a hand as well. The travellers sponsored a dance, the station broadcast the music, and listeners were invited to call in donations to get their favourite songs on the air. The money went to the TB fight. That program evolved into an annual series of amateur musical competitions staged by the travellers at various locations around the province, with a provincial final in Saskatoon or Regina. Ferguson was one of the planners behind these events, which raised millions of dollars over the years. Indeed, he was credited with coming up with the idea. Not only did the competitions raise much-needed funds, but they also gave the fight against TB a higher profile throughout the province.

The Fort San facility expanded in the years after the First World War. Ferguson continued to head the TB fight in the province through the building of sanatoriums at Saskatoon and Prince Albert. His greatest struggle came in the years of the Great Depression. Money was scarce but patients weren't. To his everlasting credit, Dr. Ferguson kept the San going, maintained standards, and kept the all-important push on for public awareness and early diagnosis of TB.

When he stepped down in the fall of 1948, Dr. George Ferguson was feted by Saskatchewan premier Tommy Douglas; by

Saskatchewan's lieutenant governor; by the Canadian Tuberculosis Association; and by the Saskatchewan Anti-Tuberculosis League. Ferguson was sixty-five, understandably tired after his long battle, but he could take great satisfaction from the progress made against TB during his tenure as superintendent of the San program.

Of course, Dr. George Ferguson was much more than a competent superintendent. His clinical research became a resource that is still relevant fifty years later. The programs Ferguson developed became models nationally and internationally. After retirement, he devoted six years to researching and writing a book called *Studies in Tuberculosis*. A professorship was established in his name at the University of Saskatchewan in 1972. Countless awards and honours bore testament to the importance of the work he had performed. Quite possibly, Ferguson's greatest gratification came when, at long last, an antibiotic treatment became available that moved the TB battle onto a whole new plane.

When he died in 1964 at the age of eighty, the battle Dr. George Ferguson spearheaded against TB had achieved a degree of success even he could never have foreseen.

The Liberals' Liberal

JIMMY GARDINER

1883 – 1962

James "Jimmy" Gardiner, MLA, cabinet minister, premier, and federal MP, had one of the longest records of service in elected office in Canada.

*J*immy Gardiner, as he was affectionately known throughout Saskatchewan, brought integrity to his work, and, in some cases, a single-mindedness not often seen in a successful politician. The biggest dam in Saskatchewan is named after him, and his name still comes up in connection with the battle to keep the Ku Klux Klan out of Saskatchewan politics, but James Garfield Gardiner is notable for a great deal more. Indeed, with one of the longest records of service in elected office in Canada, the MLA, Saskatchewan cabinet minister, premier, and later federal cabinet member Jimmy Gardiner may well have defined liberalism in Saskatchewan during his long and fruitful career.

Gardiner's roots would probably be described in modern parlance as lower middle class. Born on a farm near Exeter in Huron County in Ontario in 1883, Gardiner came from sturdy stock in rather difficult economic times. When Jimmy was only six, his parents decided to try their luck south of the border, settling in Nebraska. But after seven years they concluded that the drought and dust storms of their new surroundings were worse than life in southern Ontario, and they returned to Canada in 1896.

Jimmy Gardiner was by all accounts a bright young man and his time in the United States broadened his education, if not his parents' pocketbook. Back in Canada, he helped out on the family farm and got work on neighbouring farms when he could, receiving $12 to $15 a month for hard labour. He was well liked for his good nature and willingness, and those who remembered him commented on his love of books and reading.

Like many young people of that time, Jimmy looked to the frontiers for opportunities he couldn't see in the settled and conservative farming country of Ontario. At age seventeen, he joined a homestead excursion and travelled to Manitoba, where he found work for the winter on a farm owned by one of his uncles. He made no money but received room and board in return for his labours. By 1902, Jimmy had had enough of the life of an itinerant farm worker, and he returned to school. It was a courageous move because most young men of his age quit school early, eschewing books and learning in the hope of making a living by brawn alone. Gardiner looked elsewhere for security, and by 1904 he had acquired enough training to undertake a teaching job himself. After a year and a half, he entered the University of Manitoba where he secured his Bachelor of Arts with honours in 1911.

Perhaps Jimmy's university experience was the precursor to his interest in politics. In any event, he honed his skills as an orator and debater, earning distinction in both, along with a silver cup symbolizing the college debating championship. He led the university's international debating team and earned the highest honours of any participant when his team took on a competitor from North Dakota University. His first job after completing university was as school principal in eastern Saskatchewan. In 1911, he played a key role in the election of Liberal Thomas McNutt, the Reciprocity Candidate in Saltcoats. He made a name for himself in that campaign, speaking convincingly from the platform on behalf of his candidate. Eighteen months later he threw his own hat in the political ring. In 1913 he was nominated to run for the Liberal Party in the constituency of North Qu'Appelle, and he won handily.

So began a career in politics that spanned forty-four years, first as an MLA and cabinet minister in the Saskatchewan government from 1914 to 1935, and then as an MP and federal cabinet minister from 1935 to 1958. In 1922, Saskatchewan premier Charles Dunning made Gardiner his highways minister and minister in charge of the Bureau of Labour and Industries. When the premier stepped down in 1926, Gardiner was the unanimous choice of the party to be Dunning's replacement. As new premier, Jimmy Gardiner was a man with a social conscience, due in part, perhaps, to his long and faithful association with the

United Church. In any case, as premier he was in a position to implement some of the social measures he thought were necessary if Saskatchewan was going to be known as a place of both stable economic opportunities and compassion for the less fortunate. Gardiner kept his finger on the pulse of government by taking over the finance portfolio, in addition to his duties as premier, a crushing load for most people, but quite manageable for anyone with Gardiner's capacity for hard work.

Gardiner's term as premier was, for the most part, one of economic expansion in the province, largely due to Saskatchewan's increasing share of the international wheat market. Money markets around the world recognized the province's financial stability by according Saskatchewan a series of excellent credit ratings. But a degree of turmoil was introduced into the province's political life when the KKK (Ku Klux Klan) moved in. The 1929 election was marred by frequent clashes between Klansmen and the Gardiner Liberals, with crosses burned at several Liberal rallies. Gardiner denounced the anti-continental-immigrant and anti-Catholic Klan at every opportunity. However, he probably hurt his own cause when, without having any evidence to back up his claim, Gardiner accused the opposition Conservatives of seeking Klan support. The Klan signed up a few new members in Saskatchewan and made a splash by ranting against Catholic and Jewish immigrants who were coming into the province from eastern Europe. But the KKK influence quickly waned.

The Liberals won the greatest number of votes in the 1929 election, but the party had to relinquish power when the Conservatives and the Progressives joined forces (forerunners of the Progressive Conservatives). That sent Gardiner into opposition ranks for five years, until 1934 when the Liberals were returned to power. That year, not even one member was returned to office from the Conservative-Progressive alliance.

The following year, Gardiner was invited to become federal minister of agriculture when Mackenzie King's Liberals swept back into power in Ottawa. He was uniquely suited for that post, having gained much knowledge about the agriculture industry in the west during his time as head of the Saskatchewan government. Jimmy Gardiner's performance in his new job inspired confidence among farmers coast to coast, as he once again demonstrated his capacity for hard work. He carried an extra burden during the first months of the Second World War, serving as minister of national war services in 1940–41 in addition to his normal duties in the agriculture portfolio.

Gardiner earned a reputation for fighting for agriculture, and especially for representing the interests of his constituents in Saskatchewan. Among the stories that are told about his long service in Ottawa is the tale of the Gardiner Dam. Of course it wasn't the Gardiner Dam then, it was just a gleam in the eye of a handful of politicians and farm supporters. With bitter lessons of the Great Depression fresh in their minds, they were eager to do something to prevent a repeat of the dust bowl days in southern Saskatchewan. Gardiner had long extolled the virtues of a dam near Outlook to capture precious water in a lake, which would be used both for recreation and as a source of water for irrigation.

The most serious obstacle to the dam was in the prime minister's office. By then Louis St. Laurent had replaced Mackenzie King, and St. Laurent was far more interested in spending millions on development in his home province of Quebec. Why go out on a limb and approve the second largest construction project in Canada for a western backwater? Insiders maintain that Gardiner put his career on the line over the dam, to no avail. It wasn't until the fiery John Diefenbaker took over in Ottawa with a huge majority that real action got underway on the controversial project. It was NDP premier Tommy Douglas who insisted that Gardiner's contribution be recognized when it came time to name the dam. It was a rare moment of non–partisanship, although not one that Diefenbaker appreciated. He wanted it to be the Diefenbaker Dam and he wasn't mollified when the new body of water created by the dam was called Lake Diefenbaker. In the end, however, he took his place with Douglas and the rest to help declare the dam completed.

Jimmy Gardiner's formula for public service was obviously a winner. He won seven elections during his forty-four years in office. Regardless of what his peers said, he upheld the principle of ministerial responsibility at all times. He also believed in, and unabashedly practised, political patronage. He would not countenance the drinking of any alcoholic beverages or the use of profanity. When Gardiner left public life, political friends and foes missed him, as did the people of Canada.

One Woman's War

GLADYS ARNOLD

1905–2002

Gladys Arnold (at right, wearing a dark coat) in France
during or shortly after the Second World War.

The story of Gladys Arnold's early life is unremarkable and typical of the times, yet Gladys, from Regina, Saskatchewan, became a groundbreaking reporter and war correspondent. She was the only Canadian journalist covering events in France when the Second World War began. Not only did this courageous woman risk her own life repeatedly to keep a whole country informed about life in Paris in the terrifying days before the arrival of the German occupiers, but she also took up the cause of the Free French in their desperate underground war to liberate their country from the Nazi juggernaut.

Arnold's overseas work began as a combination of an adventure abroad, and a personal quest for firsthand information. She wanted to see for herself how different political systems operated in European nations, so she could judge the merits of socialism, fascism, and communism, all of which were subjects of such hot political debate in Depression-ridden Canada. Unemployment was a huge social problem across the country, but the prairie provinces were suffering the most. Federal and provincial governments seemed helpless in the face of growing despair.

Gladys Arnold was born in the small southern Saskatchewan town of Macoun in 1905. It was one of over a dozen places to which her father had been dispatched during her childhood by his employer, Canadian Pacific Railway (CPR). She recalled in later life that she had attended seventeen different schools in Saskatchewan, Alberta, and Manitoba. She eventually graduated from Weyburn Collegiate and Normal School, planning on a career in teaching. She taught in a number of schools in rural Saskatchewan in the succeeding years, and put in a stint as a teacher at the Success Business College in Winnipeg.

Gladys wasn't looking for the things that attracted many of her peers—husband, home, and family. Rather, with an inquiring mind combined with a tendency to push the envelope, Gladys wanted to try new things. Much later in her life, she wrote that she had made a promise to herself to "some day see every country in the world, get everything out of every day, live in the pursuit of all my life, and there make my future." A secretarial job opened up at the *Regina LeaderPost* in April of 1930, and Gladys jumped at the chance to get her foot in the door. She was not particularly interested in secretarial work, but she saw an opportunity to work her way into journalism, which would offer new challenges.

There were no journalism schools in those times. Reporters learned their craft on the job. They were picked for their curiosity, their willingness to work hard, and that certain indefinable quality that editors called news sense. Arnold was assigned to be assistant to the editor-in-chief, a job that meant everything from getting the coffee, to running his copy out to the typesetters, to collecting his suits from the cleaners. But Arnold pushed and eventually got some writing assignments. She was a fast learner, a good speller—one of the attributes old-time newspaper editors valued highly—and not intimidated by any of the requirements of the job. Soon she was writing editorials, features and news stories, and conducting interviews. Her work was good and her interviews, especially, produced interesting and insightful copy. Often her pieces were picked up by other papers.

For the next five years Arnold applied herself and made an impression on her boss with, among other things, her thorough and courageous coverage of the Regina Riot. Southern Saskatchewan at the height of the Depression was not a place of great opportunity, however, and Arnold, at thirty, did have that promise to herself to keep. In 1935, she resigned and headed for Europe, making her way by train to Churchill, Manitoba, and from there by grain cargo ship to England. She was by no means wealthy, so to make ends meet she started to submit freelance pieces to Canadian Press (CP), Canada's largest wire service and the principal source of foreign news at the time. The piece work paid very little, however, and when she was feeling the pinch,

Gladys told CP that she would have to stop submitting stories and look for a full-time job. They immediately appointed her their full-time Paris correspondent and, with the news of her appointment, included her first weekly paycheque of $15.

With her money problems resolved, Gladys Arnold began to report from all over Europe, sending stories home to the *LeaderPost* as well as to CP. Over the next four years she sent dispatches from France, Belgium, Switzerland, Germany, Austria, Czechoslovakia, Hungary, Italy, and from the Spanish border when civil war broke out in that country. Along the way, she secured her firsthand look at the various types of governance, covering stories in nations with socialist systems, with fascist regimes, and others with communist governments. To Gladys, none showed any greater promise than the Canadian system when it came to the large social problems of the day.

Back in Paris in the late 1930s, war clouds were gathering. Homesick for prairie skies and wheat fields, Gladys Arnold decided in 1939 to take a trip back to Canada. She was uncertain, as were most North Americans abroad, just what to expect as the Nazi war machine began striking out. But she soon became restless in Canada and felt the need to return to Paris, having left friends there, and not wanting to abandon her post. Canadian Press apologized, but said they were not prepared to take responsibility for her if she went back. She said she'd be responsible for herself, so CP gave her a $5 a week raise, along with their blessing.

When the German Blitzkrieg rolled into Paris in the spring of 1940, Arnold was the only Canadian reporter still on the scene. She escaped with a stream of refugees just hours before the occupying forces entered the city. It was an unforgettable experience, which she wrote about with extraordinary detail in her 1987 book *One Woman's War: A Canadian Reporter With the Free French*.

> We left Paris in the gray dawn of June 12. The shabby and shuttered buildings seemed to draw back within themselves as we passed ... Within a kilometer we ran

into a solid wall of refugees. Though we had passed many bedded down along the avenues, it was impossible to imagine what we were seeing now. An endless river of people on foot, in carts, wagons and cars; animals and bicycles so tightly packed across the road and sidewalks that no one could move more than a step or two at a time.

Later, she describes the carnage and panic when German airplanes strafed the refugee lines outside of Paris.

Gladys Arnold continued to report on the war from England, and she also helped the Free French movement. In the fall of 1940, she succeeded in getting an interview with General Charles de Gaulle, the leader who became the symbol of French resistance. That meeting sharpened her desire to help the French in any way she could. In 1942, Gladys left CP and her reporting work to promote the Free French cause. After the war, she was one of the first journalists to get back into France and witness the devastation of the years of Nazi occupation.

Gladys continued to work as an information officer for the French Embassy in Ottawa until her retirement in the early 1970s when she returned to Regina to be with her family. She established a bursary in 2000 to help University of Regina students to travel abroad to further their studies in French. She also created an academic award for a student in journalism.

After fulfilling her youthful promise to herself to "live in pursuit of all my life," Gladys Arnold died 6 October 2002. She was ninety-seven.

The heroic deeds of Saskatchewan men and women in military service in both world wars are well documented, but we know little about the involvement of civilians overseas. Gladys Arnold was one such civilian we are proud to know about.

The Grand Deception

ARCHIE BELANEY (GREY OWL)
1888 – 1938

Archie Belaney, a.k.a. Grey Owl, in 1936, when he was
back in Canada between tours of Britain.

The story of Grey Owl is one of the most enduring to come out of Saskatchewan's past. It must have been quite a sight that day in late October 1931, when Grey Owl, with his third wife, the vivacious young Indian woman he had named Anahareo, and their pets, a pair of adult beavers with their four kittens, settled down in a log cabin in a remote section of Prince Albert National Park. There would have been even more interest in this enigmatic figure if the public had had any inkling of the tortuous trail of deceit that had brought the man known as Grey Owl to such a place, and such high esteem.

Throughout history, practitioners of the art of grand deception have often been accorded places of honour in spite of their cavalier attitudes toward the truth. One such is the infamous Englishman Archie Belaney, a.k.a. Grey Owl, one of Saskatchewan's, and Canada's, earliest conservationists, and almost certainly the most controversial.

Films, picture books, and biographies have kept alive the story of Grey Owl. Public interest has seldom flagged since the mid-1920s, when Grey Owl renounced the trapping of beavers in northern Ontario and Quebec, and dedicated himself to the cause of wildlife conservation. As he began to speak publicly and write about endangered species and the need to preserve the natural world, he attracted the attention of the National Parks Service. They employed him as a caretaker, first in Riding Mountain Park in Manitoba, and then in Prince Albert National Park in northern Saskatchewan.

But it was many years, and much celebrity—through newspaper features, his own writing, and the start of his speaking career—before it became generally known that Grey Owl, the man often described in the press as a reformed half-breed, was actually Archie Belaney, the product of an upper-middle-class

English upbringing who had come to Canada as a teenager, obsessed with the notion of living like the "Red Indians" he had read about in adventure books. Biographers would come to describe his life as a "difficult puzzle," not necessarily because they couldn't accurately trace his movements—in truth he didn't really seem to try that hard to conceal his origins—but because they could never quite understand his motivation. It was entirely in keeping with the aura of mystery that surrounded the Grey Owl image that, even after his deception became public knowledge, there appeared to be little change in the popularity of his message, or his life story. Grey Owl made conservation of Canada's natural areas and wildlife a respectable, mainstream cause, in Canada and abroad. Along the way, he also became a high-profile advocate for the country's indigenous peoples.

Archie Belaney was raised by two elderly aunts in Hastings, England. He never knew his father, a drunken ne'er-do-well, and seldom saw his mother, who had given birth to him when she was just fifteen. He devoured the nature stories of Ernest Thompson Seton and adventure tales by James Fenimore Cooper. He immersed himself in any and all information he could find about North American Indians, and could not keep his mind on schoolwork, or on the succession of jobs he tried after an early exit from the education system.

Archie Belaney finally left England, a restless eighteen-year-old looking for adventure in the wilds of northern Canada. What he found was a job as a clerk at Eaton's in Toronto. That didn't suit Archie, and soon he was on the move again. He returned to England briefly, then came back to Canada. He finally found a niche of sorts, living with an Indian band in northern Ontario where he learned his first real lessons in wilderness survival. His Indian hosts enjoyed his company and there was never any question about his origins. They always knew him to be a foreigner, but appreciated that he spoke up for their rights and seemed to understand how European settlers had pushed them off their own land. Away from the band, he would go on the odd drinking spree, though he seemed likely just to strut around in an

Indian costume, his long hair in braids, carrying the kind of weapons the Indians carried. He was vague on the question of his race or nationality, telling people he was part Indian from some tribe in the southern United States. He was content to leave the impression that he really was a Native. The records are confusing. They show the often perplexing public persona of Grey Owl: the binge drinker; the domestic partner who liked women but was terrified of commitment; and the conservationist and protector of animals, who nonetheless wrote eloquently about shooting wolves.

It is known that Grey Owl had four marriages, though he couldn't seem to stay with any partner after a child came into the picture. His transformation from trapper to protector of animals precipitated a plunge into the glare of a very public conservation campaign that took Grey Owl all the way to Buckingham Palace. His move to the idyllic log cabin in Prince Albert National Park in 1931 has often been portrayed as an escape of sorts from the pressure of travel and the heavy schedule of his speaking tours. Although he was still writing and meeting the public, his touring days appeared to be over. It appeared Grey Owl was ready to settle into the quiet and security of the park for the foreseeable future.

But Grey Owl's books and articles were becoming increasingly popular. Ultimately, he was persuaded to go on the road again. He left Prince Albert National Park in October 1935, travelled to England, and undertook a grueling four-month schedule of two hundred meetings, at which it was estimated that he spoke to over half a million people. But he turned to the bottle to get through that stressful period. He went on an extended binge after his return to Canada. When he eventually found his way back to the cabin in the park, he and Anahareo decided to end their marriage. She took their five-year-old daughter and left, leaving a morose Grey Owl to his own devices.

But he pulled himself together, found another wife on a trip back east, and set about making two nature films. With that project behind him, he decided to ignore signs of ill health and exhaustion and undertake yet another British tour. He and his new wife Yvonne left in September 1937. By 23 October, he had given fifty performances at a London theatre and was booked in for another full schedule across the country. By 18 December he was back in London to give a command performance at Buckingham Palace, an event that was reported around the world. The British tour ended eight days later with what was to be a farewell broadcast on the BBC. The program never aired, however, because Grey Owl had criticized fox hunting and the BBC would not permit it.

But fame, fortune, and a long-standing weakness for alcohol caught up with Grey Owl. Back in Canada, he had to be hospitalized, and finally carried out of his cabin in Prince Albert National Park. He died in the hospital in Prince Albert in early April 1938, succumbing to pneumonia and exhaustion.

A wise and romantic figure? A fanatic visionary? The mystery remains. The precise point at which it became generally known that Grey Owl was an imposter is still part of that mystery. There was a splash of publicity back in Canada after his last tour in England in which he was accused of being a phony, but though it troubled him, it didn't diminish his popularity. Many believe that the public suspected all along, but didn't care one way or the other. He did no harm, his nature stories were genuine, his impassioned pleas on behalf of conservation were obviously from the heart, and, significantly, his Indian friends never did denounce him. So whether his dark skin came from the sun or his genetic makeup wasn't of great concern. His death was widely mourned, and after sixty years, some of his books are still in print. With his forest home preserved for posterity and his memory enshrined in literature and films, it seems that his legacy will be safe for some time to come.

Father of Medicare
EMMETT HALL
1898–1994

Emmett Hall in June 1964, two years after being appointed
as a justice of the Supreme Court of Canada.

T he Father of Medicare, a judge who distinguished himself with his devotion to the rule of law, an authoritative voice for the nation on education and transportation—Emmett Hall was all of these, and more. And he accomplished it all after what most of us think of as normal retirement age.

Hall never really retired, of course. He said with a rueful chuckle that it seemed when he'd start to relax, he'd get a phone call to carry out another assignment for the federal government. It never occurred to him to refuse. If he wasn't answering a call from the federal government, he was commenting on a development in health care for a regional or national TV news show, or giving his opinion on yet another report.

Emmett Hall told me this in an interview that I had the good fortune to have with him two years before he died at the age of ninety-six. I remember him as an animated conversationalist when the topic was in the sphere of one of his many special interests; Hall was not a person for small talk or casual discourse. Most particularly I recall how articulate and grounded he was on the issues of the day, hardly what I had expected from a man who, at ninety-four, had been "retired" for almost a decade. The day of the interview, he was incensed at the Saskatchewan government over yet another hospital closure. In typical, no-nonsense fashion, he denounced health care bureaucracies as the villain in the so-called crisis over the Medicare system. It was hardly surprising to hear him express impatience with the state of the National Health Service, with which he was so closely identified. And it was far more than just a case of pique. Hall's commitment to principles such as the one behind public health care—that it be accessible and affordable to every Canadian—reflected his strong belief in equal rights that he exemplified as a lawyer and later as a judge. As well as his work on the National

Health Care Commission in the 1960s, Emmett Hall is known for heading commissions on education and transportation, all with national implications. But Hall made his mark in Saskatchewan circles long before his commission work.

The fourth child in an Irish Catholic family of eleven, Emmett Hall was born in 1898, the son of an Ontario dairy farmer. The Halls moved west and settled in Saskatoon in 1910, in the hope of getting in on the boom they'd read about in the somewhat overstated ads that appeared in eastern newspapers. The Halls also wanted to give their children access to a university education. They'd heard of the bright future predicted for the fledgling University of Saskatchewan, still under construction on the bank of the South Saskatchewan River. The Hall family built a house within walking distance of the campus. Yet Emmett was one of only two of the eleven Hall children to graduate from the university, after a difficult five years seriously disrupted by the First World War. Teachers and students alike were fair game for armed forces recruiters. Emmett tried to enlist but was pronounced unfit because of very poor sight in his right eye. Most of the others in his thirty-three-student class did go to war, however, and he said later that had he been fit for duty, he would almost certainly have been killed. The class was decimated in one battle.

Emmett Hall had a lifelong interest in politics. One of the big events of his childhood was seeing Prime Minister Wilfrid Laurier shortly after the Hall family arrived in Saskatoon. When the Laurier entourage disembarked from the train to cheering throngs of eager supporters, Emmett and his brother pushed their way to the front of the crowd to listen to the speeches. Later, the boys climbed into the rafters of a local arena to listen to Laurier address a huge crowd. That encounter may very well have left Hall with a lifelong interest in politics. It certainly didn't turn him into a Liberal, however. Even though he failed in attempts to get elected both provincially and federally, Emmett Hall remained a staunch Tory supporter all his adult life.

Hall's law career brought him financial security as well as a reputation as a solid citizen. Although he was part of the establishment in those days, with a large and comfortable home on Saskatoon's prestigious Saskatchewan Crescent for himself, his wife, and two children, Hall was never totally an "establishment" lawyer. He believed that every accused had the right to representation and a fair trial; because of this belief, he raised a few eyebrows. In the 1930s, for example, he argued passionately as an advocate for the unemployed men charged after the Regina Riot, and succeeded in getting lower sentences for several of them.

Hall believed in giving back to his community. For many years he served on school boards and headed the board of the Catholic hospital in Saskatoon. In the latter role he worked closely with long-time friend David Baltzan, head of the top medical committee in the Catholic hospital. Baltzan was Jewish. Many feared that the two might clash over their respective faiths, yet Hall, when queried years later, just shrugged and said, "As far as I can remember, it never came up. The nuns always treated Baltzan better than they treated the Bishop." That was one of Hall's favourite jokes, and a mark of respect for Baltzan. In later life, after his retirement from the bench, Hall served for eight years (1979–1987) as chancellor of the University of Saskatchewan.

Hall and John Diefenbaker graduated from law school together and were lifelong friends, as well as sometime courtroom adversaries in their early careers. When Hall realized his own chances of ever getting elected were very poor, he directed his energies into helping Diefenbaker with his many and frequent attempts to become either a provincial Tory MLA, or a federal Member of Parliament. At fifty-eight, Hall, contemplating retirement from his law practice, wanted an appointment to the bench as a judge. However, with Liberal governments entrenched in both Regina and Ottawa, it seemed, he had all but given up on achieving that goal. That all changed. Against long odds, Diefenbaker became prime minister. One of his first acts as prime minister was to appoint his old friend Emmett Hall to the post of chief justice for Saskatchewan. (The Liberals hadn't bothered to fill the vacancy before the election, thinking they were shoo-ins for another term.)

Hall moved to the Appeal Court five years later. During his term there, he was asked by Diefenbaker to head a royal commission on health care. The first person Emmett Hall called to serve with him on this commission was Dr. David Baltzan. In 1962, Emmett received an appointment to the Supreme Court, where he served with distinction until his retirement in 1973. His own words, penned while he was a Supreme Court justice, reveal much of the credo that made Emmett Hall one of the influential figures of his time:

> A democratic society carries no inborn guarantee that it will survive on its own merits. We have seen many such societies perish, even in our time. A free society cannot be taken for granted. Truth and freedom must be guarded as precious treasures. The foundation to support the civil liberties we enjoy today is dependent upon the vigilance exercised by those who can recognize and who will protect and oppose invasion of their liberties by governments, national, provincial or municipal.

On any honour roll of individuals who made a difference in Saskatchewan and far beyond, the name Emmett Hall would certainly rank high.

Family Medicine Legends

SIGGA HOUSTON 1893–1996
CLARENCE HOUSTON 1900–1986

Clarence and Sigga Houston outside the Queen
Victoria Hospital in Yorkton in 1930.

*S*askatchewan was blessed with a good many physicians who left their mark, but few could equal the Yorkton husband and wife medical duo of C. J. and Sigga Houston. The healing sciences weren't as far advanced as they are today, but those rural healers went where they were needed, when they were needed, to take whatever expertise they possessed to the ill and the injured.

Doctors C. J. and Sigga Houston were unique to start with. Very few women became doctors in that male-dominated era. Of those who did, only a minuscule number ended up in practice with their husbands, but that was how the Houstons ordered their lives. It was a highly successful combination, both for the Houstons, and for the residents of Yorkton and area.

Sigrithur (Sigga) Christianson was born in 1893 in North Dakota, daughter of a carpenter who had brought his family to North America from a fishing village in Iceland in 1880. By 1905, the promise of free land was luring many Americans to come to Canada; the Christiansons joined the parade, settling on a farm in the Wynyard area of Saskatchewan, where they were part of a large community of Icelandic homesteaders.

Sigga, oldest of the family of four, was very interested in getting an education. Her parents were supportive, though too poor to do anything about it, so Sigga seized an opportunity to work in a boarding house in Winnipeg and go to school there. She obtained her high school education by getting up every morning at 5:00 AM and cooking breakfast for the other boarders before attending classes. She then attended Normal School in Saskatoon, becoming a teacher in 1914. After teaching for four years in rural schools back in the Wynyard district, Sigga had saved enough to finance her education at the University of Manitoba. She took a year of pre-med and was one of only fourteen women to be accepted into the college of medicine. Ten of them graduated. Well known by that time for her tenacity and diligence, Sigga was hailed in later life as the first Canadian woman of Icelandic descent, and only the fourth in the world, to become a medical doctor.

Sigga graduated in 1925. A year behind her in university was a gangly, red-haired farm boy, Clarence J. Houston, who had become her suitor. Though he was seven years her junior, which was bound to raise eyebrows if they decided to marry, Sigga was interested in Clarence. But she decided to put his affections to the test and moved to Fort Wayne, Indiana, to work in a sanatorium for a year. Apparently he passed the test, aided, no doubt, by a daily letter-writing campaign. The two were married in December of 1926.

Clarence, or C. J. as he was known for most of his adult life, was born in Ottawa in 1900. His father, a railway mail clerk, was drawn west by the same promise of free land that the Christiansons had heard. He took his family to a homestead near Tyvan, a sixty-four kilometre overland trek from Indian Head before the railroad came through. Young Clarence worked on the farm and attended a rural school until it was time for him to go to high school. He then moved to Regina, completed junior matriculation as an award-winning student, and entered the University of Manitoba Medical College, going home every summer to help out on the farm.

Sigga and C. J. set up their first medical practice in Watford City, North Dakota, but after two years they moved back to Canada to settle in Yorkton, Saskatchewan. There, C. J. developed a bustling general practice. Sigga, however, was dogged by stereotypes of the time; her professional focus was pediatrics and gynecology. She soon became known far and wide for her extraordinary ability to help sick children. That practice was her preoccupation for years, while she looked after the home and took care of their son, Stuart. She also became a prize-winning gardener. Sigga was known for her devotion to her friends.

C. J. rarely went for a whole night without being called out in those early years. He attended his patients winter and summer over a far-flung area, often resorting to horse and buggy to get through muddy roads in the spring, or horse and cutter when snow made them impassable in winter. It wasn't unusual for him to be gone for two days or more when he went on a country call. Bad roads, or severity of an injury or illness, often made it impossible to transport the patient to hospital. If the individual's condition required it, Dr. C. J. Houston would stay by the bedside until the crisis passed.

The Houstons had barely started their Saskatchewan practice before the economic crash of 1929 and ensuing onset of the Great Depression, so payment for their medical services was quite often in currency other than cash. A cord of wood perhaps, or some meat for the table would be tendered. Once a Métis man offered C. J. a bear cub as payment for his wife's maternity care. Another time he was paid with a buffalo coat, the kind made for policemen. The coat was "paid" to C. J. by a travelling salesman, who had received it as a bonus from his employer, the manufacturer. Eggs and vegetables were common as forms of compensation. But often there was no payment of any kind. Doctors of that era would never think of turning their accounts over to bill collectors. When the economy began to improve, the Houstons would send bills out, but only once a year, after harvest. If the bill wasn't paid, it was never mentioned again. As recently as 1951, Stuart Houston recalls, C. J. was charging only $2 for an office visit.

In addition to being a general practitioner, C. J. also became a respected surgeon. He always found a way to take upgrading courses to keep abreast of new developments, and he was active in the scientific side of his profession as well. He published eight papers in the *Canadian Medical Association Journal*, served as chief of staff at the Yorkton Hospital, was an officer of the Northeastern Saskatchewan District Medical Society, a member of the council of the Saskatchewan College of Physicians and Surgeons, and president of the Saskatchewan Medical Association. C. J. also co-authored one of the earliest reports to propose a form of provincial health care insurance, and served as a member of the Planning Committee on Medical Care in the 1950s. In 1959, he was invited to speak at a meeting of the British Empire Medical Association in Edinburgh, and became an affiliate of the Royal Society of Medicine.

But at home in Yorkton, this eminent medical doctor was just C. J., a member and frequent chairman of the Yorkton Collegiate Board, who once won an ecumenical award for arranging for co-operative ventures between the public and separate school systems. He was a golfer when time permitted, a curler, a fisherman, and a swimmer. He also enjoyed annual duck hunting outings on the farms around Yorkton. An avid outdoorsman and nature lover, he was the guiding force behind the York Lake Park Association, instrumental in its transition into a regional park. He then served as chairman of the Regional Park Authority, and took part in the Saskatchewan Association of Regional Parks. Also mindful of other needs in the community, C. J. guided the formation of one of Yorkton's largest retirement facilities, Anderson Lodge.

The death in 1986 of Dr. C. J. Houston was widely mourned. His widow Dr. Sigga Houston lived for another ten years, becoming the oldest living woman doctor in Canada, before her death in 1996, at 102.

In Saskatchewan, in the early part of the last century, country doctors were often legendary figures in the communities they served. C. J. and Sigga Houston were two such figures.

A Soldier's Story

HUGH CAIRNS

1886–1918

Saskatchewan soldier Hugh Cairns was the first Canadian serviceman to be awarded the Victoria Cross for Bravery during the First World War.

A great many young prairie men were among the 56,500 Canadians who died in the First World War, 1914–1918. Few performed with greater valour, or gave their lives at a higher cost to the enemy, than did a youth from Saskatchewan named Hugh Cairns, the first Canadian serviceman to win the Victoria Cross.

When the war started, Cairns was still in his teens. Born in Ashington, Northumberland, England, on 4 December 1886, he came to Canada with his family in 1911. They settled in Saskatoon, and Hugh was working as a plumber's apprentice when Britain sent out the call for Canada to join the war effort. Perhaps allegiance to the land of his birth imbued him with extra enthusiasm, but whatever the reason, Cairns was particularly enthusiastic, and by all accounts he responded over and above the call of duty from the outset of fighting.

Cairns went overseas with the 65th Battalion; he later transferred to the 46th, the Saskatchewan Regiment. Incredibly, Hugh Cairns fought in every action involving the Canadian infantry. He paid the ultimate price for his courage, fighting from his arrival in 1916 until his death just days before the guns went silent with the signing of the armistice.

Historians have proclaimed Vimy Ridge as the place where Canada established itself as a military force to be reckoned with, a nation in its own right. Cairns first came to the attention of the Armed Forces High Command in April 1917, in the legendary battle for Vimy Ridge in France. The fighting for control of the ridge was fierce, the battle plan simple. The Canadian forces simply advanced up the hill in the face of withering enemy fire. The few who survived reported the devastation of the charge. So determined were these Canadians to take the hill—where British and French forces had failed—that Cairns's regiment pressed on.

Hugh Cairns's role, in spite of his young age, was to lead a party forward to provide covering fire for the flank of his regiment. He recovered two machine guns that had fallen to the Germans in the advance, set up posts, and then repelled three different German counterattacks. He was wounded, but kept fighting until his ammunition was gone. For his deeds that day Hugh Cairns was awarded the Distinguished Conduct Medal.

Cairns received the Victoria Cross for a further action that came almost a year and a half after Vimy Ridge, just ten days before the signing of the armistice. It was just a few days after Cairns had seen his brother killed in action. Some believe that his determination to avenge that death accounted for the ferocity of Hugh's performance. Whatever the cause, General Arthur Currie described Cairns's part in that action as "a superhuman deed." The book *Our Bravest and Our Best: The Stories of Canada's Victoria Cross Winners*, by William Arthur Bishop, gives the following description of what happened:

> On November 1, 1918, ten days before the signing of the armistice, the Saskatchewans found themselves in the thick of the fighting around the town of Valenciennes, only twenty miles from Mons where the Canadian advance would end the war. In the battle, a German machine gun opened up on the platoon being led by Hugh Cairns, by this time promoted to sergeant. Unhesitatingly, Cairns picked up a Lewis gun and in the face of withering enemy fire charged the position, killing all five of the crew and taking the gun as a prize.

> A little later his unit was again stopped in its tracks by machinegun fire. Cairns rushed forward, killed twelve of the enemy and took eighteen prisoners along with their guns. But during the action he was wounded in the shoulder. Cairns ignored the pain. When the advance bogged down once more, this time by field gun as well as machinegun fire, Cairns led his party in an outflanking

movement, killing many of the enemy and forcing fifty of them to surrender.

After consolidating their position, the party, consisting of an officer in charge, Cairns carrying his Lewis gun, and two others, moved forward to reconnoitre the hamlet of Marly, where they found a yard filled with enemy soldiers. Breaking down the barnyard door, they forced all sixty of them to throw down their arms and put up their hands. But when the German officer in charge passed in front of the Canadians and got close enough to Cairns, he shot him in the stomach with his revolver. His knees buckling from pain, Cairns nevertheless shot back with a burst from his Lewis. Then a melee broke out; the Germans picked up their rifles and Cairns was again wounded, this time in the wrist. A moment later the butt of his machine gun was shattered and he collapsed from loss of blood. While a Canadian officer and soldier held the Germans at bay, others who had arrived on the scene removed Cairns from the yard.

Using a door as a stretcher, two of them began carrying him from the field. But the Germans were still inflicting casualties. They killed one of the bearers and wounded Cairns again. Finally more reinforcements arrived, forcing the Germans to surrender again. Next day, Cairns died of his wounds in hospital.

Mr. and Mrs. George Cairns, Hugh's parents, attended the ceremony at the Auberchicourt British Cemetery in France where their son was laid to rest. A street in Valenciennes was rechristened "L'avenue du Sergent Hugh Cairns" on the afternoon of 25 July 1936, the day preceding the unveiling of the Vimy Memorial. A special medal inscribed with the arms of the town was presented to Cairns's parents to commemorate the heroism of the young officer. The French Republic, at the same time, announced it had conferred the Legion of Honour upon Hugh.

Back in Saskatoon, Cairns's comrades, with the help of the community as a whole, erected a statue in a city park in his memory. In subsequent years a local IODE chapter was named in his honour, as was an armory and an elementary school. In 1977, the Cairns family presented his medals in trust to the Hugh Cairns Armory, to be put on display for the public.

The Temperance Dream

JOHN LAKE
1834–1925

John Lake and Mrs. Lake on the occasion of their
fiftieth wedding anniversary.

John Lake was a man with a dream. He had a vision of a colony of farmers and their families, happily engaged in the business of opening a new land, all united in one overarching purpose—prohibition. The plan was to call the colony site Minnetonka, until Lake heard a Native describe a local berry as "saskatoon." The die was cast; Saskatoon it was called. Although he didn't realize it, John Lake had launched the city that, a century later, would be the largest in the province of Saskatchewan, and a place where there are many more bars than there are churches.

As a Methodist minister, one would expect John Lake to be opposed to the drinking of any and all alcoholic beverages, but his opposition appears to have been more than expected. It was his obsession, and thanks to his skill as a preacher, one he was able to successfully implant in others.

As a consequence, in 1881, when he was forty-seven years old with an established congregation in Toronto, he and a group of supporters applied to the Dominion government for a tract of unbroken land on which to start a temperance colony. The request of Lake and his supporters was granted. The land would be in the North-West Territories of which Saskatchewan was at that time a part. They launched an advertising campaign that turned out to be so successful the government was unable to keep its commitment to supply all the land in one block, a circumstance that would haunt Lake and the settlers later on in the project.

Less than a year later, the company was organized. In an account he wrote himself, John Lake recalls that the organization had applications from two hundred subscribers, all committed to the cause of temperance. He was given (or he assumed) the title of commissioner, and an expedition set out in June of 1882, travelling by rail. They went to the end of rail line construction—by then in the Moose Mountain area. From there the expedition proceeded by horse and/or oxen and wagon, heading for Clark's Crossing, now known as Clarkboro, about twenty kilometres downstream from what was to become the site of Saskatoon.

What followed was a busy period for John Lake and his deputies. Lake's written account is filled with details about the religious services that were held, right down to the names of the hymns sung and the biblical text he had used for his sermon at every gathering. Lake writes: "We had our troubles every day, for we were all 'tender footers,' and it took us till the 28th of the month (July) to reach Clark's Crossing. We did not travel on Sunday. Generally we had some sort of religious service at eleven o'clock. July 30th was Sunday—a beautiful day and very warm, 80° in the shade at 11 AM. But we had preaching in John F. Clark's house." It appeared that some of the party had been left on the trail when a wagon broke down, but for the most part, the group seemed intact.

Between the lines of Lake's observances, the "tender footers" tried to get on with the business of starting their colony. That first year, Lake consulted with Moose Woods Indian Chief White Cap about a location for the colony's headquarters. The chief was helpful. He advised to choose a spot on the banks of the South Saskatchewan where the terrain was suitable and a ferry could most easily cross. The rest of the summer was spent scouting for sources of lumber to build houses, and settling the boundaries of the colony. Lake and his party then returned to Toronto, in accordance with their original plan.

They got an early start the following spring, arriving in Winnipeg in May. There, Lake arranged for a full range of building materials to be shipped to Medicine Hat; from there it floated down the river to Saskatoon. He appointed a man named S. R. Kerr to see the shipment through to its destination. Lake carried on to Moose Jaw and then north overland to Saskatoon, arriving on 29 May. He writes:

I found the Government surveyors were surveying our lands along the river and further north of the Crossing, in long, narrow strips, like half breed lands at the Red River, and as nothing could be done here [to get the government to change the survey], I started for Moose Jaw on 9th of June, and then on to Ottawa, saw the Surveyor General, Sir. J. A. Macdonald, Sir David McPherson, Minister of the Interior, and orders were telegraphed to them to lay the land out in square sections. On my arrival at Moose Jaw, on my way down from the colony I went up to Medicine Hat on the 20th of June to see Kerr and his crews and lumber. He was almost ready to start on his wonderful and perilous journey down the river. I then returned to the colony on 20th of July, found the survey of the town site progressing finely; on August 10th, it was finished, and we had a holiday and raised the liberty pole, (the longest pole we could find). Had a general jubilation, all the settlers round and from the Crossing and below to the number of 30 to 40 people. On the 27th Aug. the lumber came and we all rejoiced. Started the office and J. Lake's house and various houses, and on Sept. 20th I left for Moose Jaw again, and on to Toronto leaving a band of earnest determined people to face a cold winter and tremendous difficulties. God and the people alone knew how they pulled through.

Lake would face some difficulties of his own before long.

Because the land was not assembled in one block (as Lake had requested), it became impossible to enforce prohibition—the one defining element of the whole project. John Lake returned to the colony for about a month the following year, but was soon on his way again. "I ... left for home about the first of June, dropping all connection with the Company the following year, leaving about $8,000 of hard cash in the wreck," he writes. "I was worried by the interminable law suits, which I thought unnecessary, and unwise." Just what he meant by the term "wreck," and the nature of the suits, presumably brought by colony members, is not clear. It is known that the colony had a very basic problem, which was that the government had been unable to keep its commitment to supply all the land in one block. (As it turned out, the law suits were dismissed when a judge actually praised Lake and said if all paid up as he had done, lawsuits would not be needed.)

Lake subsequently left the ministry to become a highly successful real estate broker. The temperance colony may not have been the shining success he envisioned—its reputation for a booze-free society lasted well beyond the reality, as the city grew and new influences held sway. Lake is nonetheless remembered as a man of deep conviction, with a vision of a better world. As recently as 1958, a new public school in Saskatoon was named in his memory.

John Lake died in 1925 at the age of ninety-one, but his place in the history of Saskatchewan is assured.

Wheat Pool Crusader

ALEXANDER JAMES MCPHAIL

1883–1931

Alexander McPhail, the first president and one of the key
forces behind the founding of the Saskatchewan Wheat Pool.

*A*round 1918, Alexander McPhail and thousands of other farmers were selling their plentiful autumn post-harvest wheat at depressed prices because they desperately needed cash. Middle-men speculators were buying it up, storing it, and selling it at higher prices, making substantially more out of farm operations than farmers were making.

McPhail had seen the light several years earlier—collective farmer power through co-operative action was the only way to effectively oppose the forces of banks and grain companies, whose only motivation was profit, and whose headquarters were in the east.

In 1923, the Saskatchewan Wheat Pool was born—a farmer-owned and operated co-operative for buying and selling grain, with its own distinctive buildings for storing the grain. Alexander McPhail was the first president of the Wheat Pool, and the man regarded by many as the real force behind the organization.

My father was "a Wheat Pool man," as were all the farmers in the neighbourhood where I grew up. He was a firm defender of the Pool, and of the Canadian Wheat Board, and the whole idea of a marketing system in which farmers had some influence. He had survived the Depression, and also experienced the kind of grain marketing that was brought to the prairies by private grain companies in the years before the drought. The marketing problems of that era were frequent topics of conversation when farmers got together. I remember often hearing the name of Alexander McPhail when my father and others would recall the meetings they attended, and how McPhail would fire up a crowd of farmers with his vision of an equitable system of marketing grain.

Among my earliest memories of growing up on a farm near Kindersley in the heart of the Saskatchewan grain belt is one of accompanying my father in his old one-ton International truck when he hauled grain to the grain elevator. To me, as a child, the elevator was a fascinating technological miracle with huge "Saskatchewan Wheat Pool" lettering that could be seen for miles. A huge hydraulic lift picked up the front end of father's truck so the wheat, barley, or flax, would run out a little door in the back of the box into a grate on the floor. The elevator man warned me to never touch anything and to "never, never step on the grate," because my foot could get caught. He also showed me a spot where I could see the grain being hoisted in little scoops to some destination high up in the towering structure. He called it a "boot." He showed me a small platform off to the side called a "man lift." The lift would take him to the very top of the elevator. All the time, somewhere outside the elevator, a motor chugged away, providing power for everything that went on. That grain elevator was a tremendous symbol for prairie farmers.

When the Wheat Pool achieved one of its first objectives on 16 July 1924 by signing up over 46,500 farmers whose land represented more than 50 per cent of the wheat acreage in Saskatchewan, Alexander McPhail recorded in his diary: "Wheat Pool over the top today."

That day by no means represented the end of the struggle to turn McPhail's vision into a reality, but it was a necessary first step. Among other things, it signified to McPhail that the message he had been pounding home for several years had taken root. A combination of Alexander's earnest eloquence, along with the support of other dedicated organizers—along with circumstances that paved the way for change—caused more and more farmers to seek a radical solution to their problem.

Adversity was nothing new to McPhail. He was born in 1883 to a farming couple in Bruce County, Ontario. The oldest of nine children, Alexander and his siblings knew little but hard work from a very early age. The father of the clan was ill with TB, and finally had to heed the advice of a doctor to move west to some place with dryer air. Grandparents, parents, and children—twelve souls in all—headed for Manitoba to try to make a new start with the proceeds from the sale of the Ontario farm. The move had been left too long for McPhail senior, however. He died from TB before the first year ended in their new home near Minnedosa, Manitoba. Less than a year later Mrs. McPhail succumbed to TB as well. The responsibility for raising the young family fell on seventeen-year-old Alexander's shoulders, with whatever help his aging grandparents could provide.

Alexander filed claim on a homestead, then sold out four years later and moved to the Elfros district in Saskatchewan. When his brothers and sisters started growing up and becoming more independent, Alexander moved back to Manitoba and enrolled in the Manitoba Agricultural College, hoping to make up for all the time in school that he had lost out on as a teenager when he was working to support his siblings and grandparents.

After graduation, Alexander found a place in government service as a weed inspector. When war broke out in 1914, he undertook the job of shipping horses from western Canada to England to help the war effort. Later he joined up in the Armed Forces, but was discharged and returned, if briefly, to government service.

In 1918, he left public service to return to the farm at Elfros. The same problems awaited him there as he had experienced before the war: low prices, then speculators driving prices up. Farmers across the country were turning to political action. In Ontario the farmers' party came to power, and the newly constituted Progressive Party was gaining strength federally. A wheat board had been created by the federal government in 1917, but it was disbanded in 1919 because it was ineffectual. In the grip of post-war depression, farmers were frustrated and angry. In 1921, the United Farmers carried the provincial election in Alberta and thirty-nine Progressive candidates were sent to Ottawa by voters in the three prairie provinces. In 1922, a party formed by Manitoba farmers won a provincial election there, but the problems persisted.

By 1923, prairie farmers were ready for action, but without any real direction. Alexander McPhail came forward with his proposal for a co-operative owned and controlled by farmers. The idea caught on. Conferences were held across the grain belt, with members of the United Grain Growers, the Saskatchewan Co-operative Elevator Company, farm unions, and other groups all taking part. It was decided later that year that a contract pool would be formed, backed by an interprovincial selling agency. Along with the birth of the Saskatchewan Wheat Pool, with Alexander McPhail as its first president, a central selling agency was quickly formed, and McPhail was elected to head that as well. The first year the Pool and selling agency were in operation saw a good crop in the west, and that meant a good start for the new organization. Farmers were turning to the Pool in growing numbers. By the fall of 1928, 77,404 farmers, representing 4,344,347 hectares, had signed up to market their grain through the Pool.

Regrettably for McPhail, the stock market crash of 1929 hit the Pool hard. The organization had to turn to the provincial government for loans of more than $13 million to get through the worst of the times. But survive it did, and flourish, probably well beyond even Alexander McPhail's most optimistic expectations. He didn't live to see the recovery and what came next, but his legacy certainly did.

When my father and other farmers got together, unfailingly, one of them would express regret that McPhail died before the Pool became the largest business in the province of Saskatchewan, with the vast majority of farmers as members, and even non-members selling grain through Pool elevators which grew up in every population centre in the prairies. McPhail did get to experience the feeling of success to some degree, however, heading up the Wheat Pool and watching its steady growth and success, but he died, tragically, at a young age following an appendectomy, and didn't see the result of his hard work.

The Ham Man

FRED MENDEL

1888–1976

Industrialist and philanthropist Fred Mendel in March 1965,
when he received an honorary Doctor of Laws degree
from the University of Saskatchewan.

Fred Mendel was one of Saskatchewan's greatest benefactors and best-known businessmen. A dynamo of a man, his 1.5-metre stature cast a long shadow on two continents. Mendel was fifty-two years old, spoke little English, and had suffered terrible losses when he and his family joined a wave of Jewish immigrants who fled their homes and businesses in Europe. However, he threw himself into his new life with his customary gusto. By June of 1940 he had overcome financing and other obstacles and opened Intercontinental Packers in Saskatoon, the business that grew to become the fourth largest in Canadian meat packing circles. Fred Mendel also brought a new cultural dimension to the city and province through his love of art, his philanthropy, and his generous gift to the people of Saskatoon of the Mendel Art Gallery, along with many pieces of valuable art.

Mendel had already made two fortunes in pre-war Europe before he emigrated to Canada, buying and selling livestock, and importing Czarist currency after the Russian revolution; then reviving and operating the Europe-based meat packing business that he and his siblings had inherited from their father in Germany. Mendel secured a patent for a process for curing ham. By 1938, he had established fifteen meat packing plants around Eastern Europe. But Fred Mendel recognized the danger that the Nazism spreading across Europe posed to his family. In 1939, Mendel and his family left the Mendel meat packing empire behind and moved to New York. Finding little there to inspire them, they turned their eyes toward Canada. After living for a time in Montreal, Mendel came west. Fred Mendel found what he was looking for in Saskatoon.

Just before Mendel left Montreal and when he arrived in Saskatoon, a series of events occurred which had a profound effect on his life. "While living in Montreal," Mendel wrote in his slim 1972 autobiography, "I began to experience chest pains." Fred was under extreme stress because of the outbreak of war in Europe, the fate of his business empire, the loss of his European assets, and uncertainty about the future. He goes on to tell how he consulted a heart specialist—one of the best in Montreal—a fellow of the Royal College of Physicians and Surgeons of Canada. The specialist admitted Fred to the Royal Victoria Hospital for observation, eventually diagnosing his condition as serious heart disease. Mendel was advised to avoid heavy work and worry, bad news indeed. "It was like a sentence of death," he recalled in his memoirs.

While driving down the street in Montreal, despondent over his condition, Fred heard on the car radio the famous speech by Winston Churchill exhorting his people to "fight on the beaches, fight on the landing fields .... we shall never surrender." Mendel was rejuvenated. "My Spirits soared," he wrote. He immediately packed up his wife, Claire, and their daughter Eva, and headed west. He didn't feel as ill as the gloomy prognosis seemed to suggest. The prospect of just sitting around waiting to die was one Fred Mendel just couldn't accept.

In Saskatoon the Mendels took up residence in the Bessborough Hotel, the city's finest. Fred's wife, Claire, asked the hotel staff to call a doctor to see her husband. The manager summoned Dr. David Baltzan, thinking Mendel might be more comfortable seeing a physician who was also Jewish. "Dr. Baltzan examined me and announced that I showed no signs whatever of heart disability and that I had nothing to worry about. When I asked whether I should continue my long hours of work, he said, 'You can do anything you wish to.' I salute him as the man who restored my confidence, with advice I have honoured ever since."

But even though the lifting of the death sentence was welcome news indeed, Mendel still had lingering doubts. Which doctor should he believe? He turned to Baltzan for reassurance. Having heard of his love of horses and riding, Baltzan suggested that Mendel put his condition to the test. (The Mendels had owned a large racing stable in Europe and Fred was intensely interested in the sport.) Baltzan advised Fred to go to Banff, a place of high altitude with less available oxygen, and go for a ride. Mendel took his advice, experienced no symptoms, and returned to Saskatoon, finally convinced.

Getting his meat packing business up and running was the first goal Fred Mendel accomplished in Saskatoon. With Intercontinental Packers, the meat packing industry he started in Saskatoon in the early 1940s, Fred opened up new and valuable marketing opportunities for livestock operators all over north-central Saskatchewan. As well, with its world-class processing and access to markets across North America and abroad, Intercontinental Packers quickly became the largest private employer in Saskatoon and area.

Mendel then established markets south of the border, where his patented ham cure was a big hit. The future looked promising. But with the war in full swing, the Canadian government put a trade embargo on all meats going to the United States, a body blow for Mendel's fledgling plant. Undeterred, Mendel shifted focus to respond to the market and support the war effort, becoming a major supplier of bacon for Britain. Saskatchewan farmers rose to the occasion by responding quickly to the need for high-quality hogs to keep the plant humming.

With the end of the war, implementation of the Marshall Plan, and the creation of the United Nations, Intercontinental Packers kept its focus overseas by supplying prepared luncheon meats for starving survivors in war-weary Europe. Mendel worked through the UN's Relief and Rehabilitation Agency in that post-war effort. Meanwhile Fred began returning some of his attention to domestic markets, building on the early success his plant had experienced. The next two decades saw Intercontinental expand and grow.

Fred Mendel, dubbed "The Ham Man" by *Time Magazine*, was in a position to pursue his love of art, and, with Claire and the family, share their treasures with the community. In 1964, the Mendels made a large financial contribution to a new public facility that would build on the success of the relatively modest

Saskatoon Art Centre. The Mendel Art Gallery, located in a scenic spot on the banks of the South Saskatchewan River, was opened later that year, with a small permanent collection. The following year, in celebration of the twenty-fifth anniversary of Intercontinental Packers, Mendel donated thirteen important works by members of the Group of Seven from his own collection. That donation formed the nucleus of a collection that had grown to almost five thousand works of art by the end of the century. As well, the Mendel family continued to be the gallery's major benefactor, long after Fred had passed away.

The legacy of Fred Mendel's entrepreneurial skills and generosity live on, in Saskatoon and beyond.

Imprint of the Prairies

W. O. MITCHELL

1914–1998

W. O. Mitchell, author, lecturer, performer, stage raconteur,
and teacher, spent his formative years in Saskatchewan.

*A*lthough many people and events have put Saskatchewan on the map over its first one hundred years, the province has perhaps enjoyed its most enduring cultural celebrity from being the birthplace of W. O. Mitchell. Author, lecturer, performer, stage raconteur, teacher, and friend of a legion of fledgling writers, Mitchell made himself a presence in the life and minds of all Canadians. As odd as it may sound at first blush, one of Saskatchewan's best-known towns is one that never really existed. It's the community of Crocus, made famous coast to coast in Mitchell's fictional stories and the radio series *Jake and the Kid*, which ran on CBC Radio from 1949 to 1957. That series was a spin-off, before the word was even heard in broadcast circles, from Mitchell's signature novel *Who Has Seen the Wind*, the book that launched a literary career like no other in Canada.

Admittedly, Mitchell lived in other provinces longer than he spent in Saskatchewan, but by his own reckoning, the twelve years he spent growing up in this province were the most influential of his life. Born in 1914 in Weyburn, Bill Mitchell claimed years later that he was indelibly stained by his childhood years on the prairies. Although he went on to attend high school in California and Florida, and then lived in High River and Calgary in the foothills country of Alberta, he believed that his first twelve years—he called them his "litmus years"—had fixed his "inner and outer perspective, dictating the terms of the fragile identity contract" he would have with himself for the rest of his life.

He reaffirmed that belief when I interviewed him in 1990, just after his novel *Roses are Difficult Here* was published. He was seventy-six by then and it was unusual for him to undertake a strenuous author tour, but he was invigorated by it all, to the point that his aide and travelling companion, many years his junior, complained to me on the side that she was exhausted from trying to keep up. For W. O., the chance of getting back to Saskatchewan was a welcome break from his busy life in the East. After giving a few terse answers to questions I had painstakingly prepared about his new book, Mitchell launched into stories about Weyburn and the people he had known there. The session turned into something like one of his patented monologue performances. The story I ended up with was far different than the one I had expected, but it was an interview I'll never forget.

Mitchell had two personas, one for his family and close friends, the other for his public. His son Ormond remembered him as being aloof and introspective when he worked, but funny and approachable when he relaxed at home. Mitchell's intro-spective side appeared to develop when, as a youth, Billie, as he was known to his family, contracted tuberculosis. The disease was centred in a bone in his wrist where it developed after he suffered an injury performing acrobatics. The treatment was rest. Billie couldn't go to school, so he spent long hours tramping the countryside near the family home in Weyburn, forming a life-long attachment to the prairies and the natural world. His mother took the family to California and Florida for several winters so Billie could escape the rigorous climate of southern Saskatchewan.

After high school he attended university in Winnipeg. He hoped to become a psychiatrist but couldn't get into medical school because of his history of having TB. A trip to Europe followed, then the Depression. W. O. scraped by, surviving by working as an encyclopedia salesman, an actor, an acrobat, and a farm hand. He started writing after keeping a journal of his trip overseas, but he told no one about his literary aspirations.

In 1940, Mitchell knocked on a door in Edmonton hoping to sell another set of encyclopedias. He made the sale and also met Merna Hirtle, the woman who would share his life until his death in 1998. A few years later, with $40 to their names and their first child on the way, the two moved to High River, the scene of W. O.'s first big success with *Who Has Seen the Wind*. The publication of that novel in 1947 marked a turning point for the

Mitchells, and for Canadian literature.

As a teacher of creative writing, W. O. was fond of telling his students that "life ain't art," but in many ways his own art reflected his life. His early experiences informed his writing. *Who Has Seen the Wind* set the tone: insightful humour, but always with serious undercurrents that reflected his views on life and the society around him. Ormond recalls W. O. objecting to being stereotyped as "the old-fart prairie gopher humourist ... he would say critics missed a certain existential vision in his work, a determination to never settle for anything less than the best effort in life."

For fifty years, W. O. Mitchell was one of Canada's most popular and influential writers. The list of honours he received includes honourary doctorates from five Canadian universities, an appointment as an Officer of the Order of Canada, and being named an Honourary Member of the Privy Council in 1992.

He was a man of enormous appetites and enthusiasms, embracing people and situations with a great love of life. Known affectionately to family, friends, and fans as W. O., he spent over sixty years writing, teaching, and telling stories that epitomized the essence of what life was like on the Canadian prairies. His legacy includes, but is certainly not limited to, ten novels, countless short stories and stage plays, and a career teaching creative writing that influenced a whole generation of Canadian writers. The Mitchell name continues to be synonymous with his Saskatchewan roots, a benefit to Saskatchewan residents of immense value both culturally and economically.

Glenbow Archives NA-2306-2

Frontier Photographer

GERALDINE MOODIE

1854–1945

Geraldine Moodie was a recorder of Saskatchewan and Canadian history.

*H*ands up, everyone who has heard the name Geraldine Moodie. Chances are most can recall something of the celebrity of Susanna Moodie, the nineteenth-century Canadian writer who made a name for herself with *Roughing It in the Bush* and *Life in the Clearings*, in the 1850s. But Geraldine wasn't, and isn't, a household name.

Geraldine was Susanna's granddaughter, an important recorder of Canadian history in her own right, except that Geraldine used a camera, not a pen. Though she was obscure as a personality in the days before and after Saskatchewan entered Confederation, Geraldine Moodie's work helped reveal the vistas of the Great Plains to the outside world. Moodie's photos, with her stylized signature, appeared widely in newspapers and magazines in eastern Canada and abroad during a time of high interest in opening the west and attracting immigrants to settle there. The photo stories Geraldine left behind are fascinating. Moodie gained the trust of Natives, and so was able to get both candid photos and formal portraits of the people. She photographed such spectacles as the sun dance ceremony near North Battleford, one of the few records on film of the important religious rituals practiced by the indigenous peoples of that era. As well, the photos she took depicting family life and everyday activities in Native villages offer unique and intimate images—the kind seldom captured—for posterity.

We might never have known much about Moodie but for the determination of Donny White. While working as director of the Medicine Hat Museum and Art Gallery, White came upon some Moodie photos on display in the Old Timers' Museum in Maple Creek. Geraldine's story so intrigued him that he began to research her background, and eventually put together the book *In Search of Geraldine Moodie*, a collection of photographs and a brief account of what he found out about her life. The research turned into a four-year quest that took him all the way to the birthplace in England of Moodie's parents and grandparents. But White's work paid off in an interesting tale about a courageous and determined woman who believed in her own particular art form, long before photography became such a large part of our lives. Everywhere she lived, Moodie took pictures. Wildflowers were prominent in her work, but everything and everybody interested her. As a result, White was able to include two hundred high-quality black and white reproductions in his book about Geraldine's life.

The Toronto-born Moodie was not of frontier stock. It was only through marriage in England to a cousin, John Douglas Moodie, that Geraldine ended up on a homestead in Manitoba. Her husband gave up on farming after a time, and she found herself in the role of wife of an officer of the North-West Mounted Police (NWMP). With their growing family, the Moodies were dispatched at one time or another to almost every NWMP post in the west, and into the Hudson Bay district of the Eastern Arctic. Wherever she went, Geraldine Moody photographed wildflowers and indigenous plants of all kinds. Indeed, there is strong evidence to suggest that it was her fascination with the flora of the new land that first attracted her to photography. She set up studios at most of the posts where her husband served, often in a corner of the cramped living quarters they shared with their five children. She had to improvise darkrooms, and frequently had great difficulty getting supplies. But Geraldine persevered.

One of the Moodies' early postings was to a detachment in the Cypress Hills; over the years they returned to the area several times. When John Moodie retired from police work, they moved to a ranch in the Cypress Hills. They later moved into Maple Creek where John Moodie served as a justice of the peace and Geraldine pursued her favourite hobby, photographing prairie wildflowers. Earlier, when they lived in that area, Geraldine had shocked the locals by starting a photo studio in Maple Creek, with a branch operation in Medicine Hat. Her talent and enthusiasm turned the enterprise into a successful business—a rare accomplishment for a woman in that era, and all but unheard of in the male preserve of photography. Ever the innovative entrepreneur, she once designed and marketed photograph cards to convey Christmas and New Years greetings. By all accounts they were popular items.

Moodie was not given to keeping diaries or journals, so the story of her life is told mostly through the photo collections she left. Fittingly, White's book traces Geraldine's travels through the early west, and her life after she and her policeman husband retired in Maple Creek, through the trail of the black and white photographs she took, and preserved, over a period of some thirty years. Along with samples of her wildflower collections, the photos depict life in the NWMP, the lives of pioneers she met; such unusual sights as the ruins of Fort Prince of Wales near Churchill, and everyday activities in Inuit communities on the ice of the remote Hudson Bay. Among the most prominent in her collection is a carefully posed portrait of Poundmaker, son of the famous Chief Poundmaker, circa 1895–96.

In later years, especially after John Moodie retired and their hectic life of moving from post to post ended, and with their last move to the Cypress Hills area, Geraldine's interest centred almost exclusively on her hobby of photographing the wild-flowers of the prairie. Regrettably, little of this work appears to have been preserved. But by then she had left her indelible mark on her adopted land.

As well as the unique international success—chronicled by Donny White—achieved by this remarkable woman, Geraldine Moodie's photographs of a bygone era live on, long after her death.

Farmer, Politician

WILLIAM "W.R." MOTHERWELL
1860–1943

W.R. Motherwell: "the fighting farmer from Sintaluta."

illiam ("W. R.") Motherwell was variously known as "the fighting farmer from Sintaluta," "the statesman in overalls," and "the grand old man of Canadian agriculture." Motherwell fought for farmers' rights, and endlessly extolled the virtues of co-operative action to solve the many problems that confronted settlers on the vast northern plains. W. R. Motherwell knew those problems first-hand, as a farmer. Through all the years he served in two levels of government, he never moved away from his farm, returning there at every opportunity.

Motherwell had to overcome great difficulties in his life. He arrived in the North-West Territories in 1882, long before Saskatchewan came into being, and was a community leader in every sense of the term. He counselled other farmers to use summerfallow and other measures to adapt to the dryland farming on the prairies. Motherwell's own crop was a victim of early frost, the scourge of prairie farming, for the first two decades of his farming practice. It was his initiative that led to research projects that helped identify early maturing varieties of wheat, which substantially reduced crop losses from frost.

Born in Lanark County in Ontario, W. R. Motherwell graduated from the Ontario College of Agriculture when he was twenty-two. Those close to him expected him to return to the family farm, or to settle into a job in the public service or some private business related to agriculture. Instead, he surprised everybody by heading west in 1882 to become a homesteader. After a brief stop in Winnipeg, where he worked for the CPR (Canadian Pacific Railway) just long enough to save up the cash he needed, he headed west by oxen and wagon. Eventually, Motherwell found the site he wanted, near what would become the town of Abernethy, north of the Qu'Appelle valley. There, he built sod huts for himself and his animals, managed to break some land, and got a crop in the ground. It was his first experience with the often-hostile elements on the prairies. Like most of his neighbours, Motherwell lost his first crop to an early frost.

That loss showed him the risk associated with dependence on grain. So he went to Ontario and brought back a small herd of grade cows and a purebred Shorthorn bull. The bull was an oddity. Farmers from all over the area came to see the animal. Its fame grew after Motherwell took it to a cattle show in Indian Head and won $10 in the competitions. Neighbours speculated on how he'd spend the windfall. Motherwell fooled them all when he bought a ring and paid for his own wedding ceremony.

Ever the opportunist, Motherwell found work freighting between the CPR and the scene of the battles in the Riel Rebellion. Money was scarce. Three of every four settlers failed when they attempted to farm the virgin land of the Great Plains. And it wasn't just the elements that sent them packing. Homesteaders complained bitterly that they were being gypped by the railroads and the grain companies when they tried to market their grain. Motherwell was one of the most outspoken participants in the fight for justice for farmers. He was a founder and the first president of the Territorial Grain Growers' Association. The group eventually challenged the railway and grain company monopoly. They won a highly significant court battle that brought some relief to the hard-pressed producers.

Motherwell had named his homestead Lanark Place in honour of his home county in Ontario. The sod hut was soon replaced by a log house, where the Motherwells lived for the first fourteen years. By then, W. R. had accumulated enough stones from clearing his land to construct a stately two-storey house. He surrounded it with ornamental trees and a tennis lawn, built a barn and gave it a complete windbreak with trees, and then located a dugout in such a way as to collect as much snow as possible over winter. The Motherwell homestead has since been turned into a national historic site that attracts hundreds of visitors between Victoria Day and Labour Day. It is located three kilometers south of Abernethy on Highway 22. Abernethy is one hundred kilometres east of Regina on Highway 10.

When Saskatchewan was declared a province in 1905, W. R. Motherwell was talked into running for the provincial Liberal party, and he won his seat handily. Motherwell's career in politics was remarkable in light of the fact that he never did act like a real politician. He was often intractable, impatient with bureaucratic processes, and a thorn in the side of his own leaders. But those same leaders recognized this man's bond to the land and the people of rural Saskatchewan. His popularity never wavered, and he was always seen to be working in the interests of a better agriculture industry, something that was vital to both urban and rural dwellers in those days when success on the farms meant success and growth in business.

When Liberal leader Walter Scott was forming his first cabinet, he was well aware of Motherwell's popularity in the countryside. Scott unhesitatingly invited W. R. to become Saskatchewan's minister of agriculture. It was a courageous appointment. Motherwell was not politically astute, and his intractability frequently put him at odds with the premier and the caucus. But agriculture was crucial to the future of the province and Scott needed Motherwell's experience and integrity. Scott's strategy was successful. As Saskatchewan's first agriculture minister, a post he held for thirteen years, Motherwell created the framework of policies that turned the industry of agriculture into the economic engine of the whole province.

In 1921, Motherwell went to Ottawa to serve as federal minister of agriculture for the Liberal government of Mackenzie King, where he again made his mark. In Ottawa, once again, Motherwell proved to be an invaluable resource, with his understanding of farming issues in both east and west. He held the farm portfolio until 1930, and then served another ten years as an ordinary backbencher. He tirelessly promoted such issues as the value of education in adapting settlers to the unique demands of farming in Saskatchewan. Besides encouraging the planting of early maturing wheat varieties, Motherwell's initiative spearheaded research that resulted in the discovery of a rust-resistant strain of wheat. "Rust" is a disease that turns wheat brown.

Motherwell is remembered for many things from the years he spent with the agriculture portfolio at both provincial and federal levels of government. He was adamant that the new University of Saskatchewan should have a college of agriculture. He endlessly championed a scientific approach to farming. He believed the very future of Canada was wrapped up in the soil. He admonished farmers and others that they must "make these soils last forever." He created "Better Farming Trains." These innovative instructional trains travelled provincial rail lines, with trained personnel sharing the latest in agricultural techniques with all who would listen.

When he finally retired from politics at age eighty, Motherwell remarked, "When a man drops out at the age of eighty, people can't say he was a quitter." W. R. Motherwell's interests in issues related to soil quality, and farming in general, continued unabated until his death in 1943.

Motherwell's legacy lives on. Saskatchewan became the province with nearly half of the cultivated land in Canada and the exporter of about 10 per cent of the world's wheat. It is also the province best known for its co-operative institutions, and for an agriculture policy base that has served the people of the province well for one hundred years. The "fighting farmer from Sintaluta" would probably look upon that as a victory for the values he upheld through a long and fruitful life.

When Saskatchewan became a province in 1905 it was place of great promise, but much unrealized potential. But for the foresight and vision of a few individuals, it would have remained that way. One of those individuals was William ("W. R.") Motherwell, a man whose dedication to agriculture was phenomenal.

University Builder

WALTER MURRAY
1866–1945

Walter Murray, the first president of the University of
Saskatchewan, circa 1937, the year of his retirement.

*W*alter Murray, the University of Saskatchewan's first president, put the province on the map nationally by laying the foundations for a world-class university. It was Murray's firm belief that a university dedicated to the service of its people must be seen as the anchor for the principal industry in the area, which, in Saskatchewan, was clearly agriculture. In his view, education meant helping people, through learning, to see how to make the most of their economic opportunities, as well as how to enjoy the fruits of a wider understanding of the world. Murray did not see the institution as an ivory tower, but rather as a resource to be used by as many people as possible.

When Murray arrived from his native New Brunswick in 1908, it was in the midst of a wrangle over where the university should be located. He was to overcome this, and many greater challenges, in his lifetime of dedication to the university.

The story goes that when Walter Murray first saw the site selected for the University of Saskatchewan in Saskatoon, its only inhabitants were a pair of coyotes scrounging for a meal. No doubt that rather desolate sight confirmed for the newly appointed president of the not-yet-built university that he had been right to hold out for Regina as the home of the institution he had been hired to bring into being. But Murray was no quitter. He had been persuaded by Saskatchewan premier Walter Scott, a man who shared his own convictions on the importance of education, to undertake the gargantuan task of creating an institution of higher learning in a fledgling frontier province. Walter Murray set out to do just that.

It was a close call, however. When he looked at the various alternatives for the university site, Murray resolved that if the government didn't select Regina, he would return to the Maritimes. Perhaps it was the challenge of the raw, undeveloped site on the riverbank in Saskatoon that made him change his mind. Or maybe the once in a lifetime opportunity to build an institution from the ground up, with the sweeping mandate Premier Scott had given him, was irresistible for a man with very strong opinions on what a university should be. After all, in Saskatoon he would be out from under the eyes of government officials in Regina. Whatever the reason, Murray's decision to stay was a fortuitous moment for a province in only its third year of existence, with few resources except its sparse population and the potential of millions of hectares of productive farm land.

Walter Charles Murray was born at Studholm, New Brunswick, in 1866, the son of a doctor. He had graduated from New Brunswick University with a B.A. in 1886, conferred with just about every honour available, going on to Edinburgh University to obtain a Master of Arts with first honours in philosophy. Later he studied at Berlin University. In 1903, Queen's University of Kingston, Ontario, honoured him with the degree of Doctor of Laws. Scholars of Walter Murray's ilk were rare indeed. When Scott's recruiters decided to lure him west as their first choice to head the University of Saskatchewan, Murray had also had a distinguished twenty-year career in higher education back in New Brunswick.

But Murray was more than just a brilliant educational theorist, whose work with the university and professional organizations had brought him recognition nationally. He had also demonstrated his broad interest in community life, serving as alderman for the City of Halifax from 1903 to 1908, representative of the Presbyterian Church on a special committee about union with Methodist and Congregational Churches, and secretary of the Marine Branch of the Royal Caledonian Curling Club. Walter Murray was also a dedicated family man, with a wife and three young daughters.

The Murrays moved to Saskatoon in 1908. The following spring, land was purchased in Saskatoon, on the banks of the South Saskatchewan River. Almost immediately, Walter threw himself into the task at hand. He assembled a small faculty and classes began in four poorly ventilated and only partly heated rooms in a downtown office building, while construction got underway on the new university site. Walter Murray's vision for the University of Saskatchewan was for a large institution, with faculties of arts, science, engineering, law, medicine, and above all, agriculture. In keeping with his conviction that a university must be seen as the anchor for Saskatchewan's principal industry, agriculture, Walter Murray made sure that the first building on the new campus would be the agricultural building. That priority would set the tone for decades to come. Murray's preoccupation with agriculture did not mean that he didn't have a true appreciation for the importance of the humanities. He also held that education also meant a wider understanding of the world. Later, dentistry, pharmacy, and music would be added to the list of colleges.

Within five years, the university had 350 students, twenty-three professors, twelve lecturers, and two directors of extension work. Plans were in the works for colleges of arts, agriculture, and law; schools of engineering and pharmacy; extension work and women's work; along with two theological colleges and a Normal School in closer affiliation. Murray handpicked faculty members. He combed the ranks of large institutions in the east for the brightest and best, and used contacts he had built up over the years to assure, from the outset, that the University of Saskatchewan would have standards that would be recognized and respected throughout Canada and beyond.

Murray also brought another set of skills to his leadership that is unusual in a university president, much later known as "marketing and promotion." He reached out in a very personal way, travelling widely throughout the province, promoting the value of a university education, especially for the future of agriculture, and the importance of strong bonds between the university and the community. He believed that as many people as possible should have access to the university's resources. Along the way, he became a legend of sorts for his generous gestures. Returning from one of his country jaunts late one afternoon, he called home to say he would miss supper. He had stopped on the road to visit with an elderly man who was herding sheep. The man complained that he had no money and had run out of tobacco and tea. Murray bought some of each on his return to the city and immediately drove fifty kilometres back to the man's camp to deliver the supplies. During the Great Depression, Murray received appeals from across the province, responding when he could with small gifts of cash, boxes of second-hand clothing, or, on rare occasions, assistance in finding work. And those years were difficult for Walter Murray's own family. When the university's financial situation worsened, and he had to cut faculty salaries by 10 per cent, Walter Murray cut his own salary by 20 per cent.

The Depression was the last of a string of blows the new university had to weather. The First World War decimated the small faculty. Then came a serious recession in post-war years, followed by a period of rapid inflation, then the crash of 1929. Then, having survived the Depression, another war redirected the attention and resources of governments at all levels. Incredibly, the University of Saskatchewan thrived and grew—albeit at a perilously slow rate—during the worst of times.

Although tributes to Murray and his administration made it sound idyllic, in fact the university endured a year of internecine conflict that threatened the president's health—even his job. Murray was accused by four dissident professors in 1919 of a range of serious misdeeds, up to and including misappropriation of university funds. With a list of what eventually proved to be unfounded allegations, the four professors went over the heads of the administration and the board of governors to the provincial government. A subsequent investigation did not support their case; eventually they were dismissed. But by then the issue had become so divisive that the community had taken sides. Murray was so stressed by it all that he had a nervous breakdown and needed a six-month leave to recover his health. The incident was later described as a blip on the screen in a career that spanned almost thirty-nine years of progress. However, this crisis probably did underline one of the realities of Murray's administration, which was very much a hands-on style, with the president making most of the decisions. It was inevitable that some would find him too autocratic, even though few ever argued with his aims and objectives, or, in the end, with his many accomplishments.

Walter Murray's community service didn't stop with his retirement in 1937. He served for several terms as chairman of the board of City Hospital, and was frequently called upon to serve on national boards and commissions. He even took a hand in the legal affairs of the country, supporting the nomination of University of Saskatchewan law lecturer and board member J. W. Estey to the Supreme Court.

Before his death in March 1945, Walter Murray co-authored a history of the university that was so much a part of his life. He once summed up his philosophy in a typically straightforward observation: "Saskatchewan should have the best and the reputation of its university from the outset should be good." That dedication to excellence became the hallmark of the Walter Murray years at the University of Saskatchewan.

Métis Martyr

LOUIS RIEL
1844 – 1885

Louis Riel, an unlikely revolutionary, circa 1879,
six years before he was hanged for treason.

*C*onsidering the relatively short amount of time Louis Riel actually spent in the part of the North-West Territories that would eventually become Saskatchewan, the man made an extraordinary impact on the history of the province. His deeds, real and otherwise, as leader of the Métis forces during the North-West Rebellion, became the stuff of legends. His hanging on 16 November 1885 made him a martyr in the eyes of Métis people throughout the northwest—and of many others as well—who believed his cause was just. It was also a public relations nightmare for the faraway national government led by Sir John A. Macdonald, and a macabre ending to a sorry period in the history of the country.

We know that part of the legacy left by Riel was his symbolic act of courage in challenging the establishment, as well challenging the national government and all its resources, in a show of hopeless defiance. The outcome of the rebellion was never in doubt, but some would argue that Riel's defiance in itself may have influenced the history of the nation by sowing the seeds of a more egalitarian society. Others, however, accord Riel and his short show of resistance little importance in the grand scheme of things, some even claiming that his fate was deserved because his acts were treasonous. It's probably fair to say that in the court of public opinion, the "Riel as martyr" view has come to hold sway in recent years. Still, the debate goes on and will no doubt do so for generations to come—if for no other reason than that the Riel Rebellion was the only official civil strife that ever got to the pitched battle stage in this peaceful country. For its time, the rebellion was a huge story. It is also a tale that has been told and retold, in every form of media available. Shelves full of biographies analyze and minutely pick apart the rebellion. Military strategists have shaken their heads over the way the fighting was carried out. Social scientists have made a banquet of its true meaning. Still, though we all know the story writ large, there are questions that remain unresolved.

One of the first debates that raged after Riel's death was whether or not he was sane; that debate goes on still. In the eyes of some observers, anyone would have to be out of his mind to put a ragged band of Métis fighters up against an army representing a whole country. Among the many portrayals of Riel the man is that of a charismatic leader urging his forces on to violence. But that ignores one of the most important sources of this story: Riel's own deputy, Gabriel Dumont. Dumont steadfastly insisted that Riel held his fighters back, even to the point of jeopardizing the strategy Dumont had carefully worked out. Dumont's version of history has it that had the Métis attacked the forces of General Middleton while they were en route to Batoche, the battle could have been delayed, or maybe even prevented. But Riel would not let them attack, insisting that if the Métis acted only in their own defence, God would protect them.

We'll never know if he was right.

Perhaps we know too much about Riel as the fire-breathing defender of the rights of the downtrodden in the Red River Rebellion, and later at Batoche, and not enough of Riel before he became the lightning rod in a row over racial discrimination. If so, it may well be because a look at his pre-revolutionary days reveals very little of the man he was to become. Louis Riel wasn't an ordinary young man of his times, but he certainly didn't stand out as someone who would end his life on the gallows for treason. In fact, Louis Riel's childhood was not unlike those of many on the frontier in the mid-1880s.

Born in 1844 in a thatch-roofed house at the confluence of the Red River and a small waterway known as the Seine, Louis was by all accounts a thoughtful and bookish youngster, a charmer with large brown eyes and a mop of auburn hair. His paternal grandmother was of mixed blood, but all his other ancestors were French Canadian. The first-born in a family of comfortable means, though not great wealth, young Louis developed a social conscience at an early age. He was sorry for the poor Indian children he met as he walked to school, and often gave his lunch to one of them. His mother heard about this. Worried that he wasn't getting proper nourishment, she asked the housekeeper of the local bishop to give Louis some lunch on those days when he gave away his own lunch. The bishop got wind of the story and took an interest in the boy. Just before Louis's thirteenth birthday, the bishop gave him access to his library, and the boy would spend hours looking through tomes of philosophy and literature. The following year, the bishop announced that Louis would be awarded a full scholarship to attend a top college in Quebec. The understanding was that he would go on to become a priest. At age fourteen, the youngster, along with three other Métis boys from the settlement who were thought to be priestly material, were on their way to Montreal. It would be ten years before Louis again saw his home back in the Red River colony.

Politically, Louis's first years were influenced by conservative thought, a respect for the law, and obedience to the Catholic Church. His father was known as something of a leader in the small community, but though he spoke out for the rights of the Métis in their sometimes abrasive dealings with the Hudson Bay Company and the British, Louis's father was no revolutionary. Louis worshipped his father, as a child enjoying the older man's attention, and remembering him as someone who was always ready for a game, and one who could make the serious youngster laugh.

At school in Montreal, the young Louis Riel existed in a rarified atmosphere of constant study under an order of strict and demanding priests. His few weeks of annual holidays were spent with the family of one of his uncles; again, it was a conservative household with strict rules of behaviour. Louis immersed himself in his studies and quickly rose to the head of his class, a position he maintained through most of his four years before gaining university entrance. There, he again threw himself into the task of becoming a priest, and again excelled in his studies. He was also making a reputation for himself as a poet of considerable talent. A highlight of his years in Montreal was a visit to the city by the Prince of Wales. Louis and the other Red River boys were actually given time off from classes to attend the event. That possibly accounted for the fact that Riel always had a soft spot for the British monarchy, even though he came from a tradition of dislike and suspicion of all things British.

All indications were that Riel was on his way to becoming a priest, as the bishop back in Red River had hoped. Riel senior paid a visit to Montreal, to see his son and several members of his own family who lived in or near the city. It was the only time Louis saw anyone from home during his time at school and he was delighted to be reunited with his father. Sadly, it was the last time the two would ever be together. His father died the next year at only forty-four years of age. When the news reached Louis, he was devastated. He was depressed for months; his grades slipped, and he resolved to quit school. The dream of priesthood was dead.

Part of Riel's problem was that he worried about his family, which had grown by two more to a total of nine children in the years he had been away. With his father dead, Louis felt a duty as the oldest son to go home to help out. The Red River country was in the grip of a drought, with an invasion of grasshoppers eating anything that people did manage to grow. But if Louis was going to be of any help, he needed money. His years of study had left him with a superb classical education. He was fluent in two languages, urbane and comfortable in high society, and ready to take on the world. He was also penniless.

Louis found work as an apprentice with a law firm. Although the head of the firm was a man with an established reputation and a philosophy with which he tended to agree, young Louis was ill-suited to the work. Also, Louis had fallen hard for a young woman who was forced by her parents to turn down his proposal of marriage. They could not tolerate his mixed-blood ancestry. The young woman's decision to follow her parents' orders hurt Louis deeply. His response was to quit his job and head for

Chicago. Finding nothing there that interested him, he moved on to St. Paul, Minnesota, where he worked at a variety of jobs. While in Minnesota, he connected up with groups of Métis freighters who were hauling goods back and forth across the border. They brought him up to date on conditions back in Red River. The news wasn't good from the Métis in Canada. He probably sent money home to his mother, and managed to save a sum to help the family when he finally arrived back in the settlement in 1868. He lived the quiet life of a farmer for a few years. Then, the maelstrom of political and racial conflicts swept him along, and the rest, as the saying goes, is history.

That Louis Riel tried to work inside the system to change things for the better for the Métis is not in doubt. But all his efforts were defeated, including his attempt as a duly elected member of the federal Parliament to take his seat in the House of Commons. There is also no doubt that he did play a leadership role in the Métis defiance in Red River, and that extreme violence occurred on both sides. But the record also clearly shows the consequences of the Anglo-Saxon imperialism of that time, and the contempt shown cultures other than European.

Maggie Siggins summed up the Riel story succinctly in an epilogue to her excellent 1994 book *Riel: A Life of Revolution*. She described him as "a man who was truly a humanitarian, who gave up prestige and wealth to fight for the underdog, who led a life of dedicated revolution even though his instincts, conservative and devout as he was, might not naturally have led him in that direction."

If that description constitutes insanity, or treasonous behaviour, then a great many highly respected Canadians over the years may have committed similar offences, thankfully without meeting the same tragic fate as Louis Riel.

Premier with a Vision

T. WALTER SCOTT

1867–1938

Saskatchewan's first premier, T. Walter Scott, relaxing
from an onerous schedule and battles with ill health.

T.Walter Scott was Saskatchewan's first premier, and one of the most popular in the province's history. He was also a man with two embarrassing secrets. One concealed what would have been in those times a devastating truth about his origins. The second, ostensibly at least, kept from the public the fact that he suffered from a chronic debilitating illness of the kind seldom discussed out loud.

The secret about his origins was that Walter Scott had been born out of wedlock. That may not seem like much in this day and age, when single mothers no longer raise eyebrows and the term "illegitimate child" is seldom heard. But in 1905, when Scott won election to the highest office in the new province, public standards were vastly different.

Thomas Walter Scott was born in 1867 in rural Ontario, not far from London. As a young man he realized that his ancestry and consequent lack of opportunity meant that he really didn't have much of a future. The rough and tumble of the burgeoning North-West Territories called to him. It was a good choice. Walter Scott soon made his mark, first as a printer's devil—a combination of an errand boy and jack-of-all-trades—at a small newspaper in Portage la Prairie, Manitoba. The youth had a flair for words and respect for the power of the press, so the work suited him. When his boss moved to Regina the next year, 1886, Scott followed. By then he had advanced to typesetting and printing and both he and the new Liberal newspaper, the *Journal*, thrived in the town, then populated by nine hundred people.

By 1900 Scott had really moved up in the world and had become an entrepreneur. He had made money at land specula-tion and owned a newspaper in Moose Jaw. He was also very active in the Liberal party, speaking frequently and with elo-quence about the future for Saskatchewan as a province. He was elected that year as the member of the House of Commons in Ottawa for Assiniboia West, a constituency of the North-West Territories. He held that post until 1905 when Saskatchewan was declared a province and Scott led the Liberals to form the first provincial government of Saskatchewan.

Walter Scott's promise of "peace, progress and prosperity" sat well with the electorate. He settled in to face the formidable task of building a province. By all accounts he delivered on the promise. Scott won three elections. The first legislature had twenty-five members and a four-member cabinet. Scott oversaw the implementation of a wide range of laws. Some are intact today, such as the liquor law and school law, as well as the legislation creating municipal governments across the province. Scott's government enshrined the right to vote for women. Scott himself, with only a grade eight education, proudly set the wheels in motion to create the University of Saskatchewan. The university and the new Saskatchewan Legislature buildings were cornerstones in the provincial infrastructure that Scott put in place.

The second secret, his chronic illness, was a problem that constantly dogged Walter Scott. He was subject to deep depression. In contemporary language, his diagnosis would likely be bipolar disease, since he experienced periods of frenetic activity between bouts of depression. During those "highs" he was tireless, innovative, and charming. When he was down, he was reclusive, uncommunicative, and listless. Indeed, the condition became so serious that for much of the eleven years Scott was premier, he was actually out of the province, and often the country, for up to six months of every year. He travelled extensively and consulted medical specialists around the world during the winter months, as he found that it helped if he could avoid the cold and gloom of prairie winters.

A measure of the impact of his depression can be seen in a very surprising fact that was revealed in some old photographs: Scott actually missed the ceremony held in 1912 that opened the new Saskatchewan Legislature building. The building project had consumed him for about seven years. It was Scott's vision, and his alone, that turned the ambitious scheme into a reality. The futuristic building was financed mainly on faith and Scott's confident prediction that Saskatchewan would become a metropolis on the prairie with a population of ten million people. Yet he missed his moment of triumph. Those close to him must have seen that the pressures of the job, combined with the illness, had the premier at his wit's end. Yet no one said a word in public. Scott's absence was simply explained away with one of the usual excuses—a business commitment outside the country, or some personal business he couldn't avoid.

There were whispers, and even opposition politicians were rumoured to have had a fair idea of what was really going on. For years, Scott had travelled extensively in search of some kind of treatment that would ease his suffering, but to no avail. The only benefit was that when he travelled in the winter he could escape the darkness that often triggered his worst depressions. But politics in those days was a far more civilized activity than it was to become one hundred years later. Some things crossed an invisible line and were simply not done. For example, you just didn't take advantage of an opponent's weakness when to do so would have humiliated the opponent and his family; you would demean your own cause in the process. Scott was first, last, and always a gentleman. In those times, it would have been un-thinkable to label him a "bastard" in the press, or to allege that he was mentally ill. Besides, it was clear that the public liked and trusted the premier. He was widely seen to be virtually non-partisan, interested only in what would benefit the fledgling province and its people. And whatever the man's problems or inner fears, he was an effective politician by instinct. Perhaps his own humble beginnings made him sympathetic to the average constituent. It was a time when the common touch was a rare thing in political life; the evidence suggests that Scott's success was due, in no small measure, to the fact that he was perceived to be a man of the people.

Scott was progressive and relied very little on any ideology. He was a populist, sensitive to the wishes of his constituents and generally respected. He practiced patronage, as did all political leaders of that era, but not to excess. He campaigned hard and became known for starting lawsuits against an opponent as part of his electioneering strategy. But Walter Scott scrupulously avoided the pitfall of corruption that swallowed up many politicians in that era. During the construction of the Saskatchewan legislature buildings, Scott's political foes charged that he was getting payoffs to award contracts to certain builders or designers. He immediately ordered exhaustive investigations, all of which found the claims to be without substance. Indeed, they were shown to be frivolous. The Scotts lived in an average home with none of the trappings of the rich. Walter wisely opened his personal books to scrutiny, thus putting to rest any and all fears that he was corrupt.

Scott resigned from the Saskatchewan government in 1916, perhaps hoping in retirement to find the solution to his health problems that had eluded him for eleven busy years as the premier of a rapidly growing province. That wasn't to be, however. After moving to Los Angeles, he fell into a deep depression that lasted for two long years. His wife and one or two close friends stuck with him, but seeing him through that period was difficult. He did regain a measure of stability, however, and returned to Canada to settle down to what he hoped would be a quiet life in Victoria. He grew restless after several months of inactivity, and decided to return to journalism. He still owned the newspaper in Moose Jaw, and undertook to write two editorials a week. After a good start and enthusiastic reception from readers, Scott's writing began to raise eyebrows. He started to rehash old issues from his days in government, writing irrationally and with unaccustomed venom. It became obvious that he was experiencing mental health problems, which became much worse when his wife died in 1932.

Scott ended his days in a private psychiatric institution near Guelph, Ontario. After he and his daughter were in a car accident while driving through Guelph, a series of bizarre events landed him in jail, where he exhibited such belligerent behaviour that the local police had him examined by a doctor. When the news hit the headlines, three of Scott's former Liberal colleagues wrote to the doctor, urging him to have Scott committed for treatment. His daughter objected, but a hearing was held and the committal was authorized. Scott protested loudly, but to no avail. After two years, he died suddenly of a blood clot.

It was an ignominious ending to a life that had been widely celebrated. There has been speculation that the truth about Scott's death was never revealed. At least one researcher has suggested that powerful figures in the Liberal party helped conceal information because they didn't want either the party, or Scott's memory, to be tarnished. However, none of that takes away from Walter Scott's outstanding contribution to the building of the province of Saskatchewan.

On the grand scale of things, his somewhat bizarre personal life is not what he is remembered for. Rather, it was his skill as a pragmatic politician, his vision, and his foresight, that made T. Walter Scott successful one hundred years ago and that mark his place in history now.

Champion Wheat Grower

SEAGER WHEELER

1868 – 1961

Seager Wheeler, circa 1918, displaying two of the four
trophies he won at International Soil Products Expositions
for the strains of wheat he developed.

n 1911, an unknown farmer named Seager Wheeler, from an unknown community near a small Saskatchewan town called Rosthern, won first prize as the top grower on the entire North American continent of red spring wheat. It was a defining moment for the English immigrant.

After well over fifty years as king of the crops across the prairie breadbasket, wheat was on the decline toward the latter part of the twentieth century. Diversity was the watchword, and oilseed and pulse crops were the wave of the future. But things were different in 1911, in Seager Wheeler's youth.

A quiet man who had been turned down because of his small stature when he tried to enlist in the British navy, Seager Wheeler grew up in a fishing village on the Isle of Wight. The sea had been Seager's life, but when he couldn't realize his dream of a navy career, he turned his back on it all and set sail for Canada. He was just sixteen years old. He had made the move on impulse when he read a letter from his uncle describing his adventurous life on the Canadian frontier. Seager persuaded his mother and sister to accompany him, and the three began their adventure in Moose Jaw in 1885.

Young Seager took on any job he could find to support the family and put money aside so they could get their own homestead. Eventually he was able to float a loan of $200 from the Temperance Colony (a planned alcohol-free community), enough to buy a wagon and team of oxen, a plow, a sack of flour and some tea, and pay his entry fee on a homestead. The land was at Clark's Crossing, not far from what was then the village of Saskatoon. Another $50 loan paid for a cow.

Life was hard. The Wheeler family lived either in a dugout or a tent—written accounts of those early years don't always agree—while they built a shack. There was no crop the first year, so their diet consisted mainly of the fish they could catch in the nearby South Saskatchewan River, and the milk and cream they got from the cow. But Seager, with help from his brother (who had followed the family to the new home), cleared land and actually managed to grow two crops in the second year. But early frost destroyed most of their grain and Seager was not satisfied with the quality of the land. The Wheelers were on the move again, this time north to the Rosthern area, where they negotiated a CPR mortgage and settled on a piece of rich farmland. There the Wheeler fortunes improved, though grain growing was still in its infancy and farming was for the most part a subsistence business.

Hard work and the vagaries of weather aside, Seager Wheeler was, from the beginning, preoccupied with a search for a strain of wheat that would be especially suited to the prairies, and in particular the northern area. The strains being grown required growing seasons longer than they were likely to get on the Great Plains, and that was hampering the development of agriculture in the area. Wheeler only had an elementary-school education, and he had no idea that the development of new strains of cereal grains was generally something that happened on university campuses where men with degrees laboured endlessly in test plots. Seager knew what he was looking for and worked out his own ways of searching by selection. All Wheeler's spare time was spent walking his fields and selecting superior heads, which he saved for seed.

Seager's endless patience was paying off and he was achieving some interesting results when he first met the secretary of the Canadian Seed Growers Association, a man named L. H. Newman. Newman had heard of Wheeler's experiments and he paid the farmer a visit one day when he happened to be in the Rosthern area. The visit was an epiphany for the young farmer. Newman recalled in later years how Wheeler picked his brain and soaked up like a sponge any and all information about seeds. As soon as he could, Wheeler joined the association. Because of his interest and the work he had done, the association entrusted Seager Wheeler to be the first to test a new strain of wheat called

Marquis, and it was Marquis wheat that earned Wheeler the honours in 1911. The contest was held in New York City, and the cash prize of $1,000 in gold coins, paid by the CPR at a lavish banquet in Calgary, enabled the dryland farmer to pay off the mortgage on his land. Appropriately enough, the mortgage holder was the CPR.

Not only was this event a breakthrough for Seager Wheeler, it put the west and Canada on the map as well. Wheeler refined Marquis seed, and also developed two of his own strains. He went on to try his hand at other crops, most notably oats and barley, and then went to work on types of fruit that could be grown in the west. He had always been interested in trees and had planted various types on his own farm from the beginning. But he was especially proud of the orchard he developed. Picking and filling orders for the fruit actually became a cottage industry operated by his wife and daughters, until an extremely harsh winter came along and destroyed all his fruit trees. The loss was devastating as Wheeler had devoted twenty-seven years of careful husbandry to his orchard.

But he persisted in his efforts. Seager Wheeler won four other continental trophies as best wheat grower, including two for the strains he had developed. He published a book on his selection methods, and on farming in the west in general. That book became the most widely used in the industry. He also became a one-man extension division for the University of Saskatchewan, patiently fielding inquiries directed to him through the teaching staff. A student residence near the campus bears his name, one of many honours conferred on him over the years. Another that he treasured was an honourary law degree, conferred by Queen's University.

Wheeler retired to Victoria in 1947. He kept a vegetable garden and could once again listen to the sound of the ocean. His farm is now the Seager Wheeler Historic Farm, operated by a non-profit society. In the mid-1990s it was declared a national historic site. Wheeler died in 1961 at ninety-three years of age.

Historians widely attribute the rapid growth in the expansion of agriculture across western Canada to the development of Marquis wheat, the wheat that won the North American top wheat-grower prize in 1911 for an unknown farmer from Rosthern, Saskatchewan, named Seager Wheeler.

Saskatchewan's Literary Icon

SINCLAIR ROSS 1905–1993

Sinclair Ross set the literary standard in Saskatchewan with his 1941 novel *As For Me and My House*.

*I*f there's one Saskatchewan name that resonates above all others in literary circles in North America and beyond, it is that of Sinclair Ross. An unassuming man who toiled throughout his adult life as a banker, but whose soul was in creative writing, Ross's landmark first novel *As For Me and My House* defined the fiction genre for prairie writers and produced a stark image of Saskatchewan life.

James Sinclair Ross was born on a farm near Shellbrook in 1908. Like many young men of his time, he struck out early on his own, finding work in a bank in the southern Saskatchewan community of Abbey when he was just sixteen years old. Writing and exploring the language he loved were his hobbies and secret passions. In his mid-twenties, he experienced the thrill of seeing his byline in print for the first time as winner of a prize in a short story contest in London, England. So began a career that, for the most part, thrived in obscurity in his home country.

I had the good fortune to be granted an interview with Ross in 1993, after the Saskatchewan Arts Board had presented him with a Lifetime Achievement Award for Excellence in the Arts. He was eighty-five, suffering from Parkinson's disease and living in the Shaughnessy Veterans Hospital in Vancouver at the time. He was gracious on the telephone as he explained that his illness might make his speech unclear, but though his voice was low, he enunciated precisely.

Ross wasn't given to lengthy introspective discourses about the highly respected body of literature that is his legacy to another generation. Typical of his laconic responses to the topic of his work was his reply to a question about the theme of isolation which so permeates his stories. "Well, I was isolated. I didn't know anything about any writing community. I was only a farm boy." He was referring to the start of his writing career when, as a young man living in obscurity in rural Saskatchewan, he turned out *As For Me and My House*.

Ross said he hadn't expected the Saskatchewan Arts Board award. That was hardly surprising. The lack of recognition for his work dated back to the 1940s and 1950s when his novels and short stories went virtually unnoticed by the literary establishment. But he was pleased with the honour, and he discussed at some length the evolution of public support for writers and other artists that was simply non-existent in his time. Indeed, he said it never occurred to him to give up his work with the bank to become a full-time writer. That was unheard of for a Saskatchewan writer, and rare for any Canadian in the 1930s and 1940s.

Ross wrote because he was compelled to write. He said it was something he didn't question; it was just a need that he knew he had to fill. He wasn't even especially resentful over the fact that recognition, when it finally did come, was actually too late to do his writing career much good.

He was a good deal more animated when the discussion turned to his writing. He reflected that he still had doubts about the merits of his style and use of language. "Sometimes I'm enthusiastic, and sometimes I think I was just too trite," he commented at one point. In particular Ross said that he could still look at *As For Me and My House* and find places where the manuscript needed more work, even though he rewrote endlessly. "I never achieved the polish I wanted," he said.

His greatest pleasure came from the fact that a generation of university students had studied his work and that it was still being taught in creative writing classes. He was also gratified that his depictions of rural Saskatchewan in the years of the Great Depression had helped explain the province to the outside world.

It also pleased him that his work was being used in the teaching of English. A deep and abiding love of language was one of the reasons he wrote. It was also the reason he never could quite satisfy his own high standards. With a hint of levity, Ross said he had spoiled himself. "I can't just write something and leave it. I always come back to it, and come back to it."

With only a four-year absence during the Second World War, banking was Ross's lifetime occupation, though his vocation was his writing. Ross's output included five novels and over fifteen short stories, some of which were anthologized in two volumes.

Seven years after his short story appeared in print in Britain, it was reprinted in a magazine in New York. His first novel was accepted by a publishing house in New York in 1941, but a Canadian publisher didn't get interested until 1957. The book has been reprinted many times.

The Depression years informed much of Ross's work. The bleak social and economic climate of the Prairies was the backdrop for *As For Me and My House*, a story about a threadbare clergyman and his wife who are sent to a small prairie town. They become immersed in the social life of the community, in a story rich in language and metaphor and rife with undercurrents of sexual and psychological tension.

Ross's bank job took him to Winnipeg and later Montreal. He left there when he retired in 1968, subsequently living in Greece and later Spain before returning to Canada in 1980.

Attention for Ross's work gained momentum gradually over the years, though some who have analysed his writing and what they could find out about his life in scores of articles and books believe he was embittered by the lack of recognition when he left Canada. Ross gives a verbal shrug when I asked him how he felt about it. "I'm used to it," was his noncommittal response.

Sinclair Ross died three years after that interview, at the age of eighty-eight. His work continues to be used in creative writing and English classes across Canada.

Matriarch of the Writing Community

ANNE SZUMIGALSKI 1922–1999

Anne Szumigalski is remembered by many as the
matriarch of Saskatchewan writing.

ome years ago, after I had been book review editor at the *Saskatoon StarPhoenix* for about six months, I decided I should go to the top in local writing circles and interview Anne Szumigalski. The immediate issue was that Anne had just had a new book of poetry published, but more to the point, I felt that sharing some of her observations on her work in the context of prairie writing in general would be a useful undertaking for the local newspaper. She was, after all, spoken of with respect and affection as the matriarch of the Saskatchewan writing community.

The trouble was, I was intimidated by this literary VIP. In particular, I felt hopelessly inadequate to discuss her poetry. I was the product of twenty-odd years of refinement in the style of newspaper journalism: a genre consisting of short grunts and bursts that is the very antithesis of poetic writing.

But, needs must. The interview was arranged. As we talked— me babbling, Anne politely tolerant in her responses—it became increasingly clear that I'd have to come clean. "I'm sorry, but I just don't understand some of these passages," was how I finally blurted it out. Anne leaned back in her chair and laughed, a wonderful hearty and heartwarming laugh. "Don't feel bad," she said when she got her breath. "I can't understand it all and I wrote it." Thus was I put at ease and a conversation ensued in which I actually learned something about reading poetry, and a great deal more about Anne's years of work as a force in Saskatchewan writing circles and beyond.

Since then I've lost count of the number of writers from near and far who have volunteered observations about how they were helped and encouraged by coming to Saskatchewan to one of the writing schools at Qu'Appelle or elsewhere. Behind those schools, and often in front of a class, was Anne, along with others of the early guard of the Saskatchewan Writers Guild (such as Ken Mitchell), introducing them to the blood, sweat, tears, and intense pleasures of the craft of writing.

This early writing movement was part and parcel of an era we now look back on wistfully. Tommy Douglas and his contemporaries had made acceptable the notion that public support for the arts was just another step on the road to social justice. The seeds of the first arts board in the country had been sown and the subsequent growth blossomed into a national and provincial system envied around the world. Though its nay-sayers were never totally silenced, the public has not had a better return for its tax dollars than the Saskatchewan Arts Board grants. Over the years, these grants have supported countless writers, visual artists, musicians, and others—all the storytellers who have exported Saskatchewan on paper, on canvas, in films, and in song. In so doing, they helped arts and cultural groups in all regions of the country achieve greater maturity.

It was through the astonishing rise in the quantity and quality of Saskatchewan writing that the contributions of people like Anne Szumigalski changed the cultural landscape of the province. Her name stands out among those early builders.

Born in London, England, in 1922, Szumigalski immigrated to Saskatoon in 1951. In addition to editing and writing poetry, prose, and drama, she taught creative writing at the Saskatchewan School of the Arts from 1969 until 1980. One of Canada's most accomplished writers, she deftly managed the transition from London to a small city on the Canadian prairies, just as her work transcended any differences between rural and urban, student and teacher, mentor and friend. She was a community builder who welcomed writers of all ages into her home, where she dispensed—along with her tea—advice, support, and inspiration.

Szumigalski's skills as a writer, mentor, and teacher are legendary. She won accolades from the province and the nation for her achievements as an arts volunteer and writer: the Saskatchewan Order of Merit; the Saskatchewan Arts Board Lifetime Achievement Award for Excellence in the Arts; Life

Membership in the League of Canadian Poets; and the Governor General's Award for poetry, among others.

Anne was one of the founders of such important and enduring institutions as the Saskatchewan Writers Guild; the Saskatchewan Writers' and Artists' Colonies; the literary magazines *Grain* and *Prairie Fire*; and the Saskatchewan Summer School of the Arts. She wrote twelve books, all of which engaged the reader with innovative styles and themes that intrigued, informed, and stimulated the imagination. In particular, her autobiographical work *The Word, The Voice, The Text: The Life of a Writer*, revealed the elements of her own early life that made her the creative thinker she became as an adult. This book, written in a combination of prose and poetry, makes a lasting impression with its stark recollections of a childhood marked by the apocryphal events of the Second World War in an England under siege by the Nazi war machine.

Memories of Szumigalski and her many contributions will live on through aspiring writers. Anne was the first editor of *Grain* magazine, and her name will be enshrined in the future by the new Canadian literary prize created in her name by her successors after her death in 1999. As well, the magazine continues the tradition she began, through its emphasis on mentoring new and developing writers. Anne Szumigalski's friends in Manitoba set up an annual scholarship, to enable one Manitoba writer per year to attend the Sage Hill Writing Experience in Saskatchewan in her memory.

If the life and work of this remarkable Saskatchewan citizen tells us anything, it is that the creative process, once put in motion, is an indomitable force. Anne's legacy will live on, because it is as much spiritual as it is tangible. Through her example, and her help and teachings, generations of writers and other artists gained the confidence that comes with the knowledge that our stories are as good as those from anywhere, and that home-grown talent is as worthy of attention as that from anywhere else.

Black Settlers of Great Courage

JOE AND MATTIE MAYES 1840's–1930's

Mattie Mayes and her husband, Joe, were among a group of
black settlers who left the United States to build a new life
near Maidstone, Saskatchewan.

*J*oe and Mattie Mayes were typical of the courageous black settlers who helped open Canada's vast western farmlands. They are remembered for their achievements, not the least of which was to advance the cause of multiculturalism in a social climate that was as hostile as the land and the weather.

Whenever we think of racism or racial conflict in Saskatchewan's early history, we tend to remember the tensions between European newcomers and the indigenous peoples whose lives they disrupted. When Saskatchewan entered Confederation, the number of its black citizens was very small. But that all changed when the federal government began to invite farmers from the United States to immigrate to Canada to open up the Great Plains areas for agriculture. That invitation interested many black southerners in the United States who were still suffering under segregated social and economic conditions. The Civil War had abolished slavery, yet in many parts of the country blacks were still imprisoned by racist attitudes, and the growing power and popularity of the murderous Ku Klux Klan. Small wonder black families found the prospect of heading off into a vast land, of which they knew almost nothing, less daunting than trying to stay where they were hated and vilified. What they knew of the Canadian west was what the Canadian government's propaganda told them. The record shows, however, that government pamphlets and recruiters dispatched to find settlers didn't always tell the truth.

The offers of virtually free land in an idyllic setting, a new start in a land where everybody was equal, must have seemed almost too good to be true. We can only imagine the courage it took for these American pioneers to undertake a journey of hundreds of kilometres by horse, or oxen and wagon, with their children and all their worldly goods, to an unknown territory.

They were leaving family members, and the only lives they had ever known, to take a chance on a better future. But they were assured of nothing.

One of one thousand to fifteen hundred black families who made that journey was headed by a Baptist preacher named Joe Mayes. It was the second time Joe and his wife, Mattie—who had been born a house slave on a plantation in Georgia—had moved in search of a safe haven and a stable life as farmers. In the post–Civil War era they had fled Tennessee to homestead in Indian territory in an area that would later become Oklahoma. Joe farmed and ministered to a small Baptist congregation. However, they began to fear for their future there when the new state of Oklahoma began to introduce legislation that had all the trappings of the segregation that they had already tried to escape. In 1907, the new state legislature began to enact what were known as "Jim Crow" laws, which entrenched anti-black prejudices in state law. In addition, the power of the KKK was rising. The Mayes felt it was prudent to look for a new life elsewhere, and the Canadian invitation was the opportunity they were looking for.

The Mayes family, Joe, Mattie, and their thirteen children, accompanied by about thirty other families from their church congregation, travelled by wagon to Tulsa. From there, they were fortunate enough to be able to go by train to Winnipeg, and on to North Battleford, arriving in the spring of 1910. They decided to settle on land in the Eldon district, eighty kilometres northwest of North Battleford and twenty-nine kilometres north of Maidstone, along the Saskatchewan River. The record isn't clear on how white neighbours treated this community of black farmers, but it does indicate that at best, the west was less than welcoming. One of the Mayes's grandsons said years later that some of the white settlers in the area made it quite clear that they didn't want blacks as neighbours.

Without any kind of help, the Mayes party barely made it through that first long hungry winter. And they weren't alone in experiencing rejection. In Edmonton, when black migrants began to gather, looking for suitable farm land to claim, Edmonton's daily newspaper, its board of trade, and even ethnic groups who were themselves at the bottom of the social pecking order, joined together to demand government action against the newcomers.

A sort of public hysteria ensued. The situation was exacerbated when a young white woman in Edmonton claimed to have been assaulted and robbed of a ring in her own home by a large black man. The story spread across the country like wildfire, picking up momentum as it went, with little regard for the facts. Typical of the reaction was a headline on the front page of the Saskatoon newspaper of the day: "Negro Atrocity–White Girl Flogged and Assaulted by Late Arrivals at Edmonton." Such rhetoric substantially increased the hue and cry against the black settlers, and it was barely noticed when, after a few days, the young woman confessed that she had made up the story because she had lost the ring and was afraid to tell her parents.

The atmosphere created by such events had to have an effect on the Maidstone community, but Joe and Mattie and their supporters were undeterred. The raw prairie had to be broken, houses and barns built, and crops planted. They persevered, and by 1912 they had even managed to build a log church. The next step was to find a school where they could send their children. However, when they approached their municipal government to have school district boundaries altered to include their area, they encountered stubborn resistance. The conflict became nasty as white neighbours registered their protests against having black children attend school with their children. When the Council of the Rural Municipality of Eldon rejected the second application by the Mayes group, on the grounds that it had been improperly filled out, the group was left with no recourse but to contact the provincial education department for help. Eventually, after much foot-dragging on the part of department officials, the local politician for the district tried to get the Maidstone group the school they needed. However, what the department devised was a school district that completely segregated black families from whites. That situation existed until 1951.

Mattie became the spiritual leader of the group after Joe died in the 1930s. She served the community for many years. She is remembered for her indomitable spirit, setting off on horseback or by some horse-drawn conveyance to tend the sick, or deliver a baby.

By the 1920s about two hundred black families lived in the Eldon area. But many from the second generation preferred to try life in cities, no doubt seeking greater acceptance than they felt in their home community. But Joe and Mattie Mayes and ensuing generations of the Mayes family stayed. Now in its fifth generation, the name Mayes is still well known in the Eldon area of Saskatchewan.

Flying the Northern Bush

MIKE THOMAS 1934–2000

Bush pilot Mike Thomas in front of one of the planes
he flew across the forests and ice floes of northern Canada.

*M*ike Thomas, bush pilot, flew every kind of aircraft imaginable, often in unimaginable conditions. Thomas brought a keen sense of social justice to his work that frequently left him unhappy with what southerners were doing to the north and its people. The same spirit of independence that led him to the vagabond life of a bush pilot gave him the courage to speak out, both before and after he retired from flying. He took up writing and became known for his outspoken essays.

Long before Saskatchewan became a province, the remote reaches of its northern areas lured individuals of a certain type. They were adventurers, restless souls, almost exclusively male in the early days—men who couldn't resist the challenge of an uncharted wilderness. Cold, snow, blizzards—all the impediments of the north just seemed to add to the attraction. First these adventurers travelled the way Native northerners travelled, on snowshoes, with dog teams, or sometimes skis. They pushed back the frontiers (at times with questionable results for the indigenous populations) always acting as builders, explorers, and visionaries.

After people in the south conquered another frontier, manned air flight, it followed naturally that a new breed of adventurers would come into their own in one of the last places on earth where humans still battled the elements in very elemental ways. Air travel held the promise of opening up the north as nothing had done before. A wave of bush pilots began to make their mark, to the amazement of their more conservative peers in southern Canada. Indeed, their exploits often elicited a shake of the head from those of us who didn't feel the call to test our mettle against such hostile territory every day of our lives. But the pilots went north and became bush pilots, a brotherhood all their own. Their stories have fascinated us over the years. Their contribution to making modern Canada what it is today is a monument to the many who, in the end, gave their lives performing their labours of love.

Saskatchewan supplied its share of bush pilots, though geography was not a great consideration for such adventurers. They were as free as the birds they emulated, and the dominant qualities they shared were a love of flying and a fierce independence, not a shared hometown. They didn't see themselves as being regional, or particularly loyal to one province or territory. They went where there was work, and where that work was satisfying.

One such pilot was Mike Thomas. Born on a ranch near Calgary, young Mike got his first glimpse of aviation in 1940 when he watched hundreds of aircraft involved in pilot training for the RCAF (Royal Canadian Air Force). Mike resolved, at the tender age of six, to become a pilot. Before he was finished high school he had taken that commitment one step further, and resolved to become a bush pilot.

Thomas's career stands out not only because of his exploits flying every kind of aircraft in all kinds of weather conditions. His sense of social justice led Mike to speak out, as well as to write about, government misdeeds and the misdeeds of some of the churches whose missionaries went north to impose their faiths on northern inhabitants—who neither wanted nor needed their interference.

Thomas logged an astonishing fifteen thousand hours in the air in a career that spanned four decades. He hauled every kind of freight that moved in the north. He went where the work took him, whenever it was offered. He once told an interviewer that he'd fly any kind of aircraft that came his way. "If it would make a noise and fly, I'd fly it," he laughed. Mike also owned several different makes and models of aircraft, as well as twice owning a trading business, then a farm, and a charter business. But Mike Thomas kept moving. He even became an Air Canada pilot for a time, rising quickly through the ranks in competition with younger and better educated pilots. But though the money was good, the free-spirited Thomas had no stomach for the empire-building and office politics of a Crown corporation. He headed back to the bush, to the life he understood and with which he felt comfortable.

One of the many stories that exemplify the kind of life Mike lived is told in the excellent book *Flying the Frontiers*, by Shirlee Matheson. The same story is also featured in the gripping film on bush pilots titled *By the Seat of Their Pants*.

Not surprisingly, this story took place in winter. Thomas was flying out of Yellowknife to a remote community called Snowdrift. The superintendent of the Indian Affairs Department for the Northwest Territories, a district health nurse, and an Indian woman and her nine-month-old daughter were his passengers. Bad weather set in when they were flying over Great Slave Lake and Thomas decided to turn back. But just as they returned to the mainland, the weather really socked in. He headed for what he thought was a familiar lake to set down and wait out the storm. He put the skis down and landed on ice that was covered by a couple of cemetimetres of snow.

After determining that the ice was over twenty centimetres thick, quite safe for their purposes, Thomas and his passengers could see that they were stuck for the night and needed a place to camp. He and the superintendent started walking along an Indian trail, but they soon heard open water and realized that they were not only going the wrong way, they were actually on Great Slave Lake near a small island. They returned to the plane and Thomas started the motor and took the skis up again, intending to taxi over the ice to the island where they believed a trapper had a camp. But as they ran along smoothly, the plane suddenly began to sink. They had hit a spot of poor ice. Thomas and the superintendent jumped from the sinking craft and frantically tried to free the women in the back, but the plane had tilted when it started to sink and the cargo had shifted, pinning the women in a partial standing position with their heads against the ceiling.

Things looked hopeless. Thomas found a long pole and maneuvered it through two back windows in such a way as to slow the plane's descent into the water, then ran for shore and what he hoped would be help at the camp. But after a few strides he hit another bad ice spot and in a flash was in up to his armpits. It was twenty below with a gale-force wind and blinding snow. He pulled himself out and ran some more, hoping to get to help before his clothing froze solid and his legs quit working. Just then he met an Indian man who had heard the crash through the ice and was on the way to help, with his companion close behind on a sleigh pulled by a dog team.

With an axe he borrowed from the Indian man, Thomas chopped a hole in the top of the plane to get the women and child out. He was sure the baby was dead, but the women appeared to be still alive, though all were soaked. The Indians quickly bundled them onto their sleigh and raced for their camp, where they all crowded into one small cabin. The baby didn't die, and indeed was playing with the other Indian children within an hour. Miraculously, Thomas experienced no frostbite, though it took some time before his clothes were dry.

The storm raged for three days and the little group ran out of food, but they were all rescued when a Cessna 180 landed to pick them up. The Indian woman declined a ride to Snowdrift, but the others piled in and set out again. It was all routine to Thomas. His main recollection of the event was one of relief that it had been another bush pilot, and not the air force, that had found their partially submerged aircraft. There was fierce competition between the two types of pilots, and bush pilots often accused the air force of stealing their thunder when one of the brotherhood found a lost plane.

Thomas flew for many years after that incident, and it was a great source of pride to him that he had never been let down by mechanical failure in all the time he spent in the air. He retired unscathed and enjoyed several more years with his wife and family before he died in 2000. From the comfort of his home in La Ronge, northern Saskatchewan (a place he called a haven for bush pilots), Mike Thomas would look back on a career that was nothing short of remarkable—flying the northern frontiers of Canada.

References

Following is a list of the books I used in carrying out research for *Saskatchewan's Own*. Most are available on the shelves of Canadian libraries, and I highly recommend them to anyone wanting to know more about the individuals I wrote about, or about Saskatchewan history. I am indebted to all these authors for the work they have done to bring pieces of our past to life.

Arnold, Gladys. *One Woman's War: A Canadian Reporter with the Free French.* Toronto, ON: J. Lorimer Publishing, 1987.

Barnhart, Gordon. *Peace, Progress and Prosperity: A Biography of Saskatchewan's First Premier T. Walter Scott.* Regina, SK: Canadian Plains Research Center, University of Regina, 2000.

Braithwaite, Max. *Like Being a Millionaire.* Saskatoon, SK: Braithwaite, 1984.

Dederick, Paul, and Waiser, Bill. *Looking Back: True Tales from Saskatchewan's Past.* Calgary, AB: Fifth House Publishers, 2003.

Gruending, Dennis. *Emmett Hall: Establishment Radical.* Toronto, ON: Macmillan Canada, 1985.

Lefko, Perry. *Sandra Schmirler: The Queen of Curling.* Toronto, ON: Stoddart Publishing, 2000.

MacEwan, Grant. *Fifty Mighty Men.* Saskatoon, SK: Modern Press, 1958.

Margoshes, Dave. *Tommy Douglas: Building the New Society.* Montreal, QC: XYZ Publishing, 1999.

Matheson, Shirlee. *Flying the Frontiers, Volume 2: More Hours of Aviation Adventure.* Calgary, AB: Detselig Enterprises, 1996.

Mendel, Frederick S. *The Book and Life of a Little Man; Reminiscences of Frederick S. Mendel.* Toronto, ON: Macmillan Canada, 1972.

Miller, J.R. *Big Bear (Mistahimusqua): A Biography.* Toronto, ON: ECW Press, 1996.

Mitchell, Ken. *Sinclair Ross: A Reader's Guide.* Moose Jaw, SK: Thunder Creek Publishing Co-operative, 1981.

Murray, David R. and Robert A. *The Prairie Builder: Walter Murray of Saskatchewan.* Edmonton, AB: NeWest Press, 1984.

Shedden, Lee, ed. *A Century of Grant MacEwan: Selected Writings.* Calgary, AB: Brindle and Glass Publishing, 2002.

Shepherd, George. *West of Yesterday.* Toronto, ON: McClelland and Stewart, 1965.

Shepherd, R. Bruce. *Deemed Unsuitable: Blacks From Oklahoma Move to the Canadian Prairies in Search of Equality in the Early 20th Century Only to Find Racism in Their New Home.* Toronto, ON: Umbrella Press, 1997.

Siggins, Maggie. *Riel: A Life of Revolution.* Toronto, ON: HarperCollins, 1994.

Slade, Arthur G. *John Diefenbaker: An Appointment With Destiny.* Montreal, QC: XYZ Publishing, 2001.

Spencer, Dick. *Trumpets and Drums: John Diefenbaker on the Campaign Trail.* Vancouver, BC: Douglas and MacIntyre, 1994.

von Hauff, Donna. *Everyone's Grandfather: The Life and Times of Grant MacEwan.* Edmonton, AB: Grant MacEwan Community College Foundation, 1994.

Whelan, Ed and Pemrose. *Touched by Tommy.* Regina, SK: Whelan Publications, 1990.

White, Donny. *In Search of Geraldine Moodie.* Regina, SK: Canadian Plains Research Center, 1998.

Index